Love Redefined

By Bradly Williams

I0142504

Cover Art:

Graphic Design – Heather Smith – www.heatherbsmith.com

Potter – Darin Gehrke – www.drgceramics.com

Idea Development – Ivan Tirado – www.ivantirado.com

Photography – Bradly Williams – www.bradlywilliams.com

References made to the following:

Books:

The Five Love Languages: How to Express Heartfelt Commitment to Your Mate by author Gary Chapman – Copyright© 2007

Films:

Stripes – Released June 26, 1981 – Distributed by Columbia Pictures - Copyright© 1981

American Flyers – Released August 16, 1985 – Distributed by John Badham - Copyright© 1985

Arthur – Released July 17, 1981 – Distributed by Warner Bros./ Orion Pictures Corporation - Copyright© 1981

Days of Thunder – Released June 20, 1990 – Distributed by Paramount Pictures - Copyright© 1990

Remo Williams the Adventure Begins – Released October 11, 1985 – Distributed by Orion Pictures - Copyright© 1985

The Matrix - Copyright© 1999 – Warner Bros. – Distributed by Warner Bros.

Television programs:

Love Boat – ABC Network – Created by Jeraldine Saunders – Original Run September 1977 – May 24, 1986

Fantasy Island – ABC Network – Created by Gene Levitt – Original Run January 1978 – May 1984

General Hospital – ABC Network – Created by Frank and Doris Hursley – Currently running, in production since April 1963

Dedications

Dedicated to God, as the Father who loves me. His son Jesus as the brother who walked with me and His spirit as the well, which sprung up with the Father and Son's love combined with grace. His spirit, who loved me enough to live inside me when I was impossible to live with, impossible to love, and did not always love any of God in return. Jesus, thank you for your willingness to stand between our Father and me, so that we could meet.

To my wife of 4 years when I began this and of 6 years when I completed it. Lisa, you truly are my one true love. Thanks to God, that we both know now what love is. To quote our favorite band, Air Supply, "You're every woman in the world to me." You truly are a Proverbs 31 woman.

Finally, to my mom, Marilyn, my dad, Don and my sister, Donetta as well as friends and family and those unaware that they have been part of the process of showing me love, how to love and God's tools to show me what love is. My father was a wonderful sounding board for me in his final years and many inspirational moments came from special conversations with my sister.

As you read this, you are reading a book that is an account of my personal story. You are reading what I have read, heard, and learned. You will see where I was and where I am. That, I hope, will be enough to encourage you, to redefine love in your life.

Find out more: www.bradlywilliams.com

Contents

Prologue by Michael Waddell

The First Page

Prologue by Michael Waddell

As I sit here in my little office in Martinsville, VA trying to write a fitting Prologue for my friend Bradly and this fine work you're about to read, I pause. I pause because my office has a window that looks out on a busy mezzanine that is often crowded with people consumed with the work of the day. But today I have watched couples coming and going, some holding hands, others arguing, some just sitting in silence sipping their coffee. I see a mom with her kids, trying to keep them under control. I see my wife and my son walk through on their way to our loft on the top floor. I see those who think they are in love, those who love blindly, and those whom I love with my whole heart.

I see these people and I wonder aloud, after all I'm in my office and they can't hear me, "Those couples want to be 'in love'. Do they know what it is? That mom loves her kids even though they make her want to pull her hair out, how does she do it? Why does my wife choose to spend her days with a man like me? How does my son know that I would die for him out of love?"

In the pages that follow this poorly written prologue Bradly dives into love head first. I laughed, I cried, I learned.

Jesus told us to love one another, to go the extra mile. I've often struggled with the reality of what this truly meant then and means now, today. Heck, most of the time I don't love myself, how am I supposed to love others? In today's world, the word love has been prostituted to mean whatever pleasures our fancy.

Love Redefined is a book for our generation. I have known Bradly for six years now and as his friend I can say he lives what he "preaches". He loves his city, he's passionate about his friendships, and he loves with total abandonment his wife Lisa and their beautiful baby girl.

Bradly and I worked together for almost three years. I can't say that there was an immediate friendship. I was a young punk kid who thought I was the next superstar of Christian teaching, and Bradly, in my opinion, talked too much. But as I watched this man who sat in front of me I saw commitment and dedication, I saw passion and perseverance. And over time, I saw that while I was busy blowing smoke out my backside, Bradly was consistently meeting his goals and setting new ones.

After a year or so, Bradly and I, along with a few buddies started an accountability group at the local pub. I went mainly for the beer and stogies, but we became close. Sharing the things we struggled with, our hopes, fears, dreams. It was definitely a time that defined our friendship and also a time where we forgot about machismo and simply became men longing after God's best for our lives.

I share this because two things remained constant in Bradly's conversation, His desire to remain pure and love his wife with everything he had, and his unquenchable desire to see the people of New York City know "true love". His hope was that he and his wife would be able to go and share this love, a love that God had revealed to him only a few short years earlier.

I don't know why Bradly would ask me to write the introductory pages of his book, but I can without a doubt tell you why I agreed to write them. Bradly is a man who seeks to deliver love in all he does, and that's the kind of man everyone should be able to call friend.

Michael Waddell
Founder/President
The Table Inc.

10

The First Page

I have called this simply, "The first page" because it is just the beginning of what I hope to be a journey down a path of change. My vision is that you will open your mind to a new line of thought on an old word. Interestingly enough, by the end, you may find that, in fact, it is more an old line of thought and that this word's definition has simply been redefined once already over time. It's now time to take back love by giving it back its rightful definition.

Today, as I sit and write this particular section, my wife and I are celebrating our fourth anniversary of marriage. This may not sound like much of a milestone to some of you and to others reading this it may sound very impressive. If you're wondering why I'm writing this page today at this moment instead of celebrating, well, it's because of our celebrating that I realized I had to write this page now, in the moment and not a day later.

Celebrating the moment is one of the great things about life. It is one of the most amazing choices I have found we have. No matter how small or how big the moment is or represents it is ours to do with as we see fit and as God allows. Then there is respect. Respect for another to celebrate the moment. When you have respect for another you give them the space to celebrate the moment and when appropriate you include yourself and as that person sees fit they will include you. Celebration of life's moments and respect between two persons to celebrate, for me, I see love in that.

And that, that is why I had to write this part of this book, another book about love, today, now, in the moment that it was experienced.

CHAPTER 1

It's never to late to learn, so don't wait to learn

I have to admit, I wish I would have learned the definition of love a long, long, long time ago. Sure I heard the usual definitions from comments like, "The way you love that sport isn't the same as love for family." Or, "You love that girl as much as you're capable based on the length of time that you've known her and based on what you know thus far about her." I got that there were different types of love. It was clear there were different phases of love. However, I was still never provided with the definition of love. I just had to sort of figure it out along the way. It seems love is an assumed, understood word. It's like the sky is blue and then you go oh, anything that color is blue. But it isn't that simple is it?

When someone follows up the sky is blue and the wind blew my hat off, we aren't like *what*, a color knocked your hat off or do you mean that the sky is like the wind? Nope, that's easy. We get that there is more than one blue/blew. We know you can talk about a shoe on your foot, the kind the Old Woman in a Shoe lived in, and to shoo a fly like we sing in a child's song. The latter shoo has nothing to do with killing a fly with your shoe though you might use a shoe to shoo a fly. My point, I hope is clear. While love, is left unclear. The definition of the word is not as simple as looking at the context it falls into and coming to the conclusion, "Oh, that's what they mean."

I've seen soap and sit com stars say I love you. I have friends who tell me I love you, co-workers say I love you, and of course our family says I love you. Boy/girlfriends of two days say I love you. People scream it to rock and sports stars and many times they say it back at concerts or in a press conference and my wife and I say I love you. So how is each I love you different? What makes love, love? How can you recognize true love? These are some questions I hope to help you find the answers to as we explore this mysterious word, Love.

As I write this book I've hit my mid 30's. I would say I was provided with a true definition of love and an understanding of the word as a word and as a verb about 7 years ago. It was a strange time in my life. I had been married already twice and while I said I loved and was told I was loved, rarely did I really feel it was circulated in my relationships. Later, I met someone of whom I thought I loved. I, as they say, I fell in love. We'll talk about that phrase a little later on. However, if you're curious as to which direction I go with that, think more on the word, 'fell' than the word 'love'.

This was a very emotional relationship. Very relaxed and very fun. A lot of excitement and attraction. You see as a writer and a romantic I grew up also enjoying the soaps my sister would watch during babysitting hours. The late night shows like Love Boat and Fantasy Island and as I got older the many great, fun and romantic adventurous movies I would watch. I had prayed prior to this relationship, in despair due to my marriage before it, "Lord, why can't we live like those in movie and TV relationships." Again, we'll touch more on media and its influence in my life a little later.

I told God that, "I want to have a relationship that's exciting and full of passion" and so on. I wanted as I put it, "to live like they do in the movies!" I was tired of it just being a discipline, a sort of business relationship. I was tired of what often seemed to be a one-sided romance with an occasional response. You see this was all prior to my knowledge of Gary Chapman's Love Languages and God's word about Love. It's amazing what happens when you take some good psychology with the word of the one whom they say, "is love" and combine them. I was actually telling my wife recently how I could have been a much better husband and leader of the house and better influence in the lives of those women whom with I had had serious relationships with if only I could have seen about them and me then what I can look back and see now.

I did get to have that storybook, rather television or movie romance. See, to me story books are more like journals that can go on and on without end. What I got about 8 years ago was instead comparable to that which I prayed for, 'one like the movies!' It was amazing for about 3-6 months. Then we struggled. I couldn't understand it. As we both realized the way our lives were pulling us in directions away from that emotional side and into a reality of how our interests and passions pulled us away from one another, we began to fall apart. Eventually the relationship ended drawn out with a lot of pain and, I know for me, it left emotional scars. I began to think that this definitely could not be how love was intended to feel. This can not be how the result of love is supposed to be either. So, while dealing with a deep depression from what was incredible loss I had a new prayer.

It went something like this, "Lord, I realize now that the movies are how they are because they only have to last two hours. We never see the ending. When the guy in the difficult marriage leaves his wife for the woman who seems to really care and the wife has an affair that makes it easier for him to leave and they've both moved on and somehow are still friends and are happy... the movie ends."

But in real life the story doesn't end there. It's more like a story book or a journal. The journey that is our life continues and along with it, so does its baggage. So I asked that God would show me what real love was about. I figured clearly I had no clue.

I had three serious long term relationships over the course of ten years and all had failed regardless of how different each girl was. Regardless of my intentions or circumstances going in, regardless of how much money we had or didn't have. What had not changed was me. I was the same for the most part I figured in all of them. So I reasoned that maybe if I could better learn about love, then, as when we are better educated and begin to implement that knowledge in our lives, we change. Maybe I could change my definition and from that change, get a different result. If I could change and love correctly, maybe then, I could love as love was intended and who knows, maybe even find someone willing to love me the same way.

And as you've already read I did, and five years later we're going strong. Actually we just found out we'll have a baby to love very soon as well. Thanks God. Thanks for teaching us how to love one another through your word and books and teaching and real lives of those you've also directed.

Notes:

CHAPTER 2

Where do we get our answers?

From the information that we study.

When you think about that question, "Where do you get your answers?" Do you think of a response quickly or do you seem a bit stumped by such a question. Let me try asking this, Where do you get your answers for such questions as, "What car should I buy? Which college major should I choose? Where should I go on vacation? Where will I go to buy this or that? Which brand of '____ ITEM' is the one for me?"

Now I'm assuming the responses came more quickly. I should purchase the car that will get me the most attention or the one that will last the longest or drive best in the snow or will fit my family of five.

I will choose the major that fits my talents and interests or I will pick the one that provides for the most opportunity.

I will go to the place I've always dreamt of, _____ (Fill in the blank). I remember watching that documentary on Italy and now I think I will go. I will determine what I can spend, how long I can go and choose from there.

I will read consumer reports and reviews of the product. I will test the product and talk to others who own the product.

You see, for many questions in life we are given some sort of guide or direction or possibly instruction or tools for finding the 'right answers'. But with love many of us were given none of these answers. Or what if what information we were given to help us find our answers was way off. Like the brochure for that 'quaint' hotel that turned out to be an old run down house. What if people raved about Hawaii but when you got there, you found no waves, dirty water and a bunch of dead trees? Ask yourself how you would feel if everyone told you how great a certain vehicle was and all the non-bias reviews agreed and were consistent for years so you purchase such a vehicle only for it to break down on you multiple times shortly after purchasing.

I know I would feel cheated, lied to, and would be angry and bitter at everyone for lying to me. What about the false advertising of how wonderful that place is? I spent all my money and the little vacation time I had, only to go and return more miserable and stressed than before I left. You see when we are given the wrong information, we end up getting the wrong result. Let's look at it another way...

Where do you get your answers? From those things which we have studied through our lives. Say for example what is 2 + 2? Maybe, what is a noun, a verb, an adjective? What do you do when you have a cold? *Who or What is God.* What does the word love mean? Stop right there.

Think about it. Where do you get your answers? For math, from my math teachers. For the English questions, my English teachers. My mom and dad taught me what to do when I got a cold so that I could feel better. And for love, let's observe those who taught me the answers to the everlasting question, "What is love?"

Love; what is love. It's fascinating when you think of how we perceive love starting at an early age. When we get a spanking, we hear, I/We do this because we love you, whack! We listen to Barney sing "I love you, you love me." I often wonder why is it our children are often hearing more about love from a fictitious purple dinosaur than from real life people. Then there are soap operas, or those wonderful dramatic Spanish novellas. All the people, or at least the successful ones in their television life with money and love, seem to look perfect and even the ones who don't are somehow made cool in their imperfections. Those, however, are only but a few. After all if you had a whole bunch of 'Cool to be different' people it wouldn't be so cool any more would it?

I grew up with an older sister. Her excuse for watching Sesame Street was me and she was my excuse for watching Luke and Laura on General Hospital as they sat behind a hay bail declaring their love and the value of being on the run together. My sister was my excuse to watch such a glorious portrayal of love. My two favorite late night shows, being a product of the 80's as I am, were Fantasy Island and The Love Boat. These shows, looking back, remind me a bit of a good advertisement for Las Vegas tourism, "What happens on The Love Boat or on Fantasy Island, stays there." People always showed up a little uncertain but left with a smile.

What happened there, whether good or bad, always seemed to teach them about love no matter how realistic or unrealistic it might have been.

So sure, I've been referencing a lot about the sway of the media so let's take a closer look at my immediate influences. There was the couple who I looked at as they'd love like no other but fight like no other. A mixture of anger, passion, and giddiness like teenagers one minute and bitter like old trapped and beaten dogs the next. Ah, this must be what they mean when they say relationships take work or a good marriage takes a lot of work. Hate and love go hand and hand… don't they? I watched a girl say what seemed like almost every day, "I'm in love. I met a boy. He's going to take me here or he gave me this so I know he really likes me!"

Ah, now I was getting it. In the real world it's kind of like the television shows. You do sing I love you, he or she loves me and it's because of some giddy feeling you get inside that is aided by what a person buys you or does for you in a tangible visible sort of way. GOT IT!

A matter of fact almost all of the relationships around me resembled this clear picture of Yin and Yang but it was Love and Hurt, I can't really use the word hate but anger, bitterness, pain causing actions make the word hurt fit well. So these were my examples of love and so I went with it for years and years. I based every relationship on these experiences and these examples.

We actually have a lot of very bad love teachers all around us. The magazines that teach us about love are no where near as effective as the magazines that give us information on the best products, restaurants and stores.

CHAPTER 3
Calling a spade a spade and It is what it is

Have you ever heard these phrases? To call a spade a spade means very simply to not beat around the bush about something and just be honest. You can not call a lion a kitty cat. It's a lion, King of the Jungle. It rules, it leads and places terror in even some of the largest animals on earth! Do not try to tell me when we visit the zoo or go on a safari, "It's just like my Marshmallow, just a sweet little kitty." To say such a thing would not be truthful. It certainly isn't calling a lion a lion.

Another well known phrase is, "It is what it is." I once had a boss and as well, later, an employee who both used this phrase for everything. In some cases it didn't even fit the bill at all! Still, nonetheless, I've never liked the phrase. After all, what else could anything actually be other than, WHAT IT IS? I guess we can look back at the lion analogy. Some people see things differently and some don't always have it right. Like people who have been know to say a lion is no different than a cute cuddly kitty. Sorry, but again that isn't right. And, just in case you think I have bitterness for animal analogies, I'll happily use something else to make my comparisons. I'll use an example of myself, and how based on the information I grew up with I 'got it wrong'.

Small cars are not known for their smooth ride. Growing up, my family generally owned two types of vehicles: trucks and small cars. Often it was an older model in either case and the car was usually sporty. Neither ride smooth, period. Some do more than others, but sit inside a luxury sedan and then tell me that the sports car and truck rides smoother and you must have built in butt shocks! Still, the case was that a close friend of mine, Gene, used to own this 12 year-old Buick four door sedan when at the time, I had a 12 year-old Nissan sports car. He loved his because it was practical and he could haul around lots of stuff and lots of people and even though the oil was blacker than crude mixed with mud and I'm not sure the shocks were ever replaced it rode smooth like Buicks are known for.

I just saw an old grey sedan. My car was cool. It looked cool and it was fast so I looked cool and I was fast. In my mind it rode fine. Eventually, Gene bought a newer model sedan. I thought this was fitting. It was today's version of what he already had. It was nice, but he was in his 20's still and I didn't get it?

Gene was my radio buddy. We had both grown up dreaming of working in the radio biz and now we finally did, both DJ's for competing stations and soon to follow we were working together. I eventually assisted him in starting an overnight program. Gene was more hip than his sensible comfortable sedan might lead one to believe. He could spin records with the best of the club jocks and he had a voice that put mine to shame.

So, there came a day when we were still working on how to start a new radio venture, the one that ended up being an overnight Christian rock and metal program. A road trip ensued. Another followed that one and another after that. Gene handed me the keys one trip on the way to Dallas from Tulsa and said, "I'm a bit tired, you drive." I wasn't used to people letting me drive their cars. Most people I knew back then were pretty attached to their cars. So this took me a bit by surprise.

You can always tell a lot by sitting in different areas of a vehicle. It's good to look at the engine and the trunk. You want to know where the basics are and how hard it'll be to change a flat. How much storage you have and where the fuse box and oil gauge is, that kind of thing is important. Then go for a ride in the backseat. See how others will feel when they ride along. Take a ride in the passenger seat. How will your 'first mate/navigational officer' feel? How accessible are the cup holders, map holders, and controls for the passengers?

Now, it's time to be the captain. Take a seat in the driver's bucket seat…ohhhh, that's nice. Place your hands on the wheel, how does it feel? Take a look around, mirrors, controls, seat adjustments and of course radio dial all in place and at hand with ease. Now take off. What a ride.

I had felt how smooth this car was in the passenger seat for weeks but driving it was like driving a cloud compared to mine. I loved my car, it was fun and it was fast and it was most definitely cool for me at 18. However, I suddenly realized why Gene always told me mine rode like a wheelbarrow. At that point I realized that I liked how mine rode because I was conditioned to do so. It was what I knew the most. It was what I found comfortable because it was what I was familiar with. It was not the best riding type of vehicle and neither were the trucks I rode in. No more was that the case than if one were to say I can haul as much in my sedan as you can in your ½ ton pickup! You can haul a lot with a good sedan but it isn't going to be as much and it isn't designed to be a ½ ton pick up.

My point is this: we are conditioned in many cases into arguing with someone about the answer to something or our belief in something much like I used to argue that my car rode nicely and smooth and just as good as Gene's two sedans. When something is all we know, not only do we make it right in our minds, we also have a hard time ever letting anything else replace that information because it makes what we believe wrong. It means we must renew our thinking.

When we have believed something is good for so long, even when it isn't, we still make it good and argue it to be good because it's all we have known and seen and it works. It works until someone finally hands us the keys to something better and says, "Now you drive."

>>>I have heard, God is love, God loves everyone, For God so loved the world. You know God loves you when you're going through trials and pain and you know God loves you when you've been blessed and your prayers have been answered, by answered these people always seem to be referring to when God answers yes and we get what we want and we think is best. How do you perceive love when you think of God?>>>

Needless to say, while I had some very good friendships and some very typical, amazing, "loves of my young life" during my teenage years, truth be known, looking back I wonder how many of them I loved or loved me for that matter. Many of these people I am still very close to, many have gone their way and I mine and chances are neither path the twain shall ever cross again. In my first genuinely significant relationship I was 18 and I was "in love".

This phrase has always fascinated me. It fascinated me in the same way that most 12 year-old girls plan for their wedding at such an early age. As a kid I'd lie in bed in my room listening to the great love songs of Air Supply, Chicago, and George Michael. To be in love, what did it then and what does it now even mean? If love is a feeling, then it can be compared to being in pain, or being hot or cold, or scared. I've decided you can make someone hot by turning up the heat but they still have to choose to stay next to the fire. You can make someone afraid however, you didn't afraid them.

I'm going to attempt to quote a line from one of my favorite movies, "Remo Williams, the Adventure Begins." "Fear is just a feeling, you feel hot, you feel cold. Fear can not kill you."

The man saying this is training Remo who will be a mercenary for a top secret government agency. He is having him walk along the edge of a roof of a very tall building and he can see the fear, not only on Remo's face but in his entire body language. The fall could kill him but the fear could not. Fear is just a feeling so he had to rid himself of this.

So is love something that is just emotional? Is love something that is as fleeting as fear? If I stand safely at the center of the top of a building I feel safe. If I stand on the edge I feel afraid. For years love was a bit like this in my life. It was safe in one place, scary in another, exuberating in another. It was really just a matter of who I was with and how they made me feel and in a sort of way of speaking, where I stood and where we stood in proximity to one another.

CHAPTER 4

My first love

So this is how it began. My first love, we'll call it a crush, was with
Adrianne in 1st grade. I remember standing in line behind her at the
age of five and she was wearing a pastel horizontally striped
sweater, blue, pink and cream. It looked so soft. You know out of
that kind of fabric that you touch and go, "Wow, that is soft…"
We had already established our relationship by communicating
through subtle grins and such that we liked one another and I
believe we may have even said it. I'd venture to state that my
memory recalls that we held hands! Gasp, I know and in first grade
mind you! It's true. I was a "playa."

Wait, wait, we're talking about my first love. Let's start again. My
first love, puppy love as they call it, was when I was only ten years
old in 4th grade. At the risk of sounding too much like Charlie
Brown, it was the "Little Red Headed Girl." She was my first (kiss);
you know the really fast kiss on the lips that is both _ohh ahh_ and
ewww weird all in one. If I remember correctly, we played all kinds of
peek-a-boo games and shy hee hee teasing like you do at that age.
Actually from what I've recently observed when watching guys
attempting to pick up girls at the local pubs, not much has changed
for many even after so many years. Finally, it happened. We kissed
or we touched lips once and didn't know what to do next, so we did
nothing. Last I remember we were holding hands and skating at the
local rink. Hey, it was the early 80's in a small town and that's what
you did.

More 'loves' of the sort would come, as I would fall in love
regularly. Each one would mean a little more than the one before
but I don't remember any kissing after that for quite a while. And
so we'll skip past my other skating partners. Though I will say
during a fifth grade heart break I was forced to call Adrianne.
Don't ask me how, but I'll never forget asking, "Do you know who
this is?" (We'd only written a few times over the years) and she
replied, "Bradly?" If that wasn't glue for my broken heart… but is

that love?

So, some of you are in tears, others of you have gotten some wine to go with the cheese to help you read along. I completely understand. I'm just telling it how I remember it. Enjoy your wine. Some of you are saying, none of this is love at all, it is just what we all go through as we grow up and learn about attraction. To those, I say thank you for deep insightful realization, now stop and reflect. This would be a good time to pop some popcorn, put on a pot of coffee or tea. Don't worry, I'll be here when you get back and so will the other person reading, the one with the wine.

Actually, my first love; my first love must have been in fact when I was fourteen. I remember my first kiss on the park bench in the park of a small town in Oklahoma. No not like the kiss with the little red headed girl. This was the real think like the ones on The Love Boat or better, Fantasy Island. Yes, this park was my own Fantasy Island. I could swear in the background, was Mr. Roarke smiling as was Tattoo and they sipped a fruity drink with an umbrella. Of course had it been Fantasy Island, I would have left two days later to go home to a trivial life with no girlfriend.

It was amazing and I knew by the feelings I had inside; You know the ones, queasy, excited, nervous, on top of the world and something that at the time I couldn't describe as more than, "WOW"; I knew by this that I must be "in love". This is how it had been shown to me so it must be what it is. It had to be love right, since I did not have to leave the Island? I mean the next day she was still my girlfriend, my first REAL girlfriend.

And so it went, we followed suit immediately. From the starry eyes and embarrassment of entertaining the interest we had in one another. It began with a note. It always does at that age doesn't it? She wrote me letting me know that her favorite song was Whitney Houston's 'How will I know". This was a shy innocent way of her letting me know she liked me. I was supposed to, in response, give her an answer. And I did, eventually, with a note in music class, two rows down and three seats over, back to her that asked, "Do you want to go with me?" Check yes or no. She said yes and hence that was my first 'relationship'. We would yell when we didn't agree with one another, then our hormones kicked in and we would kiss and make up. We would give each other the silent treatment when we were jealous then we'd be back to holding hands when we did something nice for one another. Some say love is forever. I remember seeing it all over the place. There it was in greeting cards, on school folders and book covers and in songs and movies and TV shows and out of the lips of anyone who was 'in love' even if for but a day.

<<<*Amazing how we use love, something that is supposed to be good and pure to justify a reason for anger, jealousy, fighting and even lying. I remember believing that if you love someone you'll fight someone. That was an adage of many 80's songs, TV shows and movies and I remember hearing many friends and family members talking in such away in regards to love as well.*>>>

Notes:

CHAPTER 5

If you want love, you must fight for it...

Funny I thought later about fighting for love. It usually came when two people like one person. You fought to win them. Who wants to have to fight to win someone's love? That should have been an early red flag but it was not. I mean if you are fighting to 'win' something that says to me that just as easily when you let down your guard and run out of ammunition you could lose the battle. If you lose enough battles you're apt to lose the war. The WAR we call LOVE!

Wait, war and love as synonyms, can that be right? Sure. You have to fight for love. I don't think we actually got this entirely wrong. You do have to fight for love but it isn't another person you should be fighting. It is not with the one that you want to be with nor is it with the one who wants that person in addition to you. The fight that really is going on is the one inside you.

I learned much later in life that love is a choice and from what I can tell if I have to fight another man to win a woman's love then she is not choosing to love me at all. I simply won her over. If we win someone did they choose to love us or was it simply a result of our doing more than the last person, another person or than what they think the next person will do?

When you think of relationships in this aspect, think how often you've heard things like; Relationships are a lot of work. You have to fight for your man. You're going to have to work hard to get her. These seem like common place comments in the world of love. Don't get me wrong loving isn't always the easiest thing. After all, to love someone else means to take the magnifying glass off myself and place it on someone else. Several things happen when we place the magnifying glass on someone else.

One thing that happens is it makes them big to us. Sometimes they become the biggest thing in our lives. Sometimes they become too much and start to consume our lives. We start to think so much about them we don't think about much else. We stop thinking of others in our life, we stop working so hard at our job, we stop doing those things we loved doing before this person came along.

In a sense we change who we are. When this happens we aren't being true to ourselves. We become someone else. We are no longer the person who fell in love with this other person nor are we the person that they fell in love with. Now think about how dangerous this is. If we both change and if we then don't like who we are when looking at ourselves or one another then we start struggling and the relationship becomes work, a fight to make work.

The only fighting I have ever seen important to do for love is to fight to overcome the struggles in ourselves. To fight this world when it tries to pull you away from loving as we were intended, that my friends, is fighting the good fight.

I'd like you to contemplate the following. What if we continued on being the people we were supposed to be and intertwined our being with another instead of simply morphing into an entirely different being altogether.

Earlier we discussed love being a choice. However, if you win someone in a battle with someone else or even in a sort of under the surface battle with the very person whom you hope to be with that means you have to put up a fight, you must be ready for a sort of love-war. And, how do you win someone over?

First of all you need the best weapons and you need a lot, I mean A LOT of ammunition. For example, some of your weapons might be a nice car, nice clothes, and a good job with a good title. Ammunition includes, money, smooth words to smooth talk, more knowledge and more abilities, gifts and the like.

When you fight for something, obtaining it is a victory. When you think of fighting for something, or gaining anything through battle, what do you think of? I think of war for a piece of land, fighting over a place. I think of a boxing match, ah yes, this is a wonderful depiction of love. You may end up battered and bruised but eventually someone will throw in the white flag or someone will get knocked out and then everything is fine, that's just how love is.

I think of any sport that is physical and where there is a championship, generally with a trophy given to the winner. In the case of war, the victor is also given control of the enemies land. This is an even worse analogy when thinking of fighting either for love or love being a fight. Think how often you've seen people complain about someone else being too controlling. Is this a coincidence?

CHAPTER 6

Falling in love... sounds painful

Looking back at whenever I've fallen in love, I recently realized one of the downfalls that brought a strain on my relationships. When I would meet a girl, I'd usually come across with a certain confidence. Whether it was in my ideas, my lifestyle, my dreams, or whatever, there was confidence. This confidence gave them faith in me that I could lead when they needed a leader that I could support dreams when they needed support and that I was going somewhere.

Over time however, I'd become less confident. I'd pour more and more of myself into pleasing the other person which took time, energy, and such from those things which strengthened me before. Want to know part of why I'm writing this book. I really enjoy writing. I used to write a lot. I actually wrote my first book in 4th grade. Funny, right after that is about the same I started liking girls. Hmm? What I'm saying is, I need this. It's something that makes me who I am. When I'm who I am not only am I happy but I'm the man my wife loves to love. Then it's like a snowball effect. Nothing quite like **a big snowball of love.**

Many times I talk to young people about this subject. Some are in relationships, some are not. Some have more experience, some less, some happy and others hurting. One thing I tell them all is to make sure that they are not more interested in knowing the other person than they are knowing that each of them know themselves. You can get to know a person really well but if who they are is a lie then you will not know them at all.

You can easily both fall for and be someone who is fallen for as a person who is lying to those around you. Maybe you say you can do something you know if confronted you really could not. Maybe you say you really love rap music when really you just happen to like that one Snoop Dog song a lot but haven't listened to rap music in months.

Be honest with yourself, be who you are, always working to improve yourself and let others see the true you. This way when someone does make the choice to love you they won't be choosing to love someone else in the process. That can start a reverse snowball. One that keeps falling apart until nothing is left.

Another important thing that we have to make sure of when we start to fall for someone is that we do what we say and say what we mean. I remember saying I wanted a home when I met my wife. I was lying. I do want a home, when I'm like 80 I think. I want an apartment in New York City. It's true. Homes are a lot of work. Not like relationships are a lot of work. Like, physically you always have something to improve or fix or upkeep or replace or you get the idea. Then there's stuff to put in the home. Decorating for every holiday. Don't get me wrong. I'm not going to debate the right or wrong of these things. I actually love decorating for the holidays. Halloween and Christmas are my favorites!

However, I love experiencing life. I've rarely found any place in the world that you can experience life quite like New York. I want to go to a baseball game, a Broadway show, walk and ice skate in the park and write at my favorite local coffee shop. I'll choose this over fixing a toilet, putting up a fence, sanding a deck, landscaping work and saving for a new roof any day. I hate to admit it but while I enjoy having the space of a home in the suburbs and I like being able to grill out on the deck and play volleyball in the backyard I don't find equal value for the effort put in so that I can do and have those things. So, when looking back I wish I would have been more honest with myself, so I could have been more honest with my wife. Instead this has been a difficult issue and rightly so.

Remember how my first love and I started. Strangely enough my relationship with my wife started in a similar way. Through code words and a subtle shy conversation we determined to pursue something more than friendship and let down the walls that apply in those cases.

And another thing

Here's another thing to think about regarding falling. How often does 'falling' represent something good? It is quite rare to hear someone say, "Oh I just fell into that money" or "oh I just fell into that situation." The fact is even when someone inherits money they still have to choose the right way to handle it, even when someone gets a phone call that someone who knows someone they know said they were good at a skill and this person would like to interview them or give them a job, well you still have to choose to work hard and do the job well to keep it. And it was the choices you made, that the person you know saw, that made them believe you were worth referring.

I've been lucky enough to help a few persons I know get work and it has never been only because I knew them. I saw in them specific skills, talents and abilities that made me believe they would do a job well. That and that alone is why I provided them a job, a name, or referred them to someone. Sure, I've passed on information for many but it is only on what someone has actually shown me that I will refer them or provide them with a job.

My point is, you may fall into love, meaning that in a very non-ordinary, almost accidental, unexpected way you may find the person whom you will spend your life. With most people I know did not know their spouse their whole life. Instead they saw them at a bar, got googly eyes over one another and in that couples case one person still had to choose to go speak to the other and from there it was a series of choices beyond the emotions that came from that time of first sight and stars in the eyes.

The ones like myself that I know that met over the internet either because they were looking or simply just sort of wasting time and trying to make a few friends in the process have to make the effort in many cases to go a distance to meet the person. They still have to put effort into really getting to know the person, online, by phone and/or through a few meetings. Even if it seems unintentional, there's a whole lot of intentional that follows that first online message.

How about the two people who meet in the produce section when their hands go for the same apple? Or what about those two people who try to go through the empty elevator's door at the same time? Sure these types of situations happen and people meet by chance but let us say they fell into knowing the one they chose to love and not they suddenly fell into love.

After all would you rather someone end up loving you and call it an accident or would you rather say someone chose you over all others to give love to?

Think about that.

CHAPTER 7

Needy or just wanting to share those things you love with someone?

I've found that some of us just love to share the things we love with someone else. I'm guilty of this. Preferably we want to share experiences with those who also enjoy these things or at the very least can respond enthusiastically when doing them with us. I have learned that this can quickly cause us to think that we have found love when we have found something different of which I don't have a name for yet. After all in some cases you may or may not be attracted to the person or have any further interest other than to share these things, however when you begin to become connected through sharing these experiences the feelings and emotions can be construed as love.

I have said that feelings should come from love and not the other way around and this is an example as to why. I have learned something further from all of this analyzing of the subject of love. I have learned that you can change how you think but you can not often if ever change how you feel or your emotions. It is much easier to decide you are not always going to believe that something is a certain way for example, change a habit, than it is to actually change how you feel about something. Many times something happens to us to cause a change in how we feel. But how often have you had to make the determination about how you were going to think while it took an outside action to change how you feel.

Decide on a 110 degree day outside in the sun that you are not going to feel hot. Decide that you're not going to feel pain when you stub your toe. Difficult to do. However, I can determine how I think about a 110 degree day and make it more bearable but I'm still going to be hot. I can decide not to scream and curse when I stub my toe, but that doesn't mean it doesn't hurt, but strangely, like the heat analogy it does seem to become more bearable.

When you're in a position where you have feelings of attraction, connection, or along the lines of which we've spoken for someone, yet it is not a situation where you would choose to 'love' them in actions for a commitment of life as we think about love then you can in fact decide how you are going to react when you feel attracted to them.

You can tell yourself not to think in a manner that makes it more difficult. To love someone else in action, you can even change how you will respond to things they do however, when you feel attracted, when they show up looking good, or when they say something or you connect about something of similar interest that you know you both wish you could share together, in fact you can not stop what you will feel. It just happens. First the emotion erupts and then the feeling is created; now you react. The final part is the only part of this scenario which you have much control over and with the first three things happening regularly around one another, it is difficult not to give up on the effort of what you think and how you react now and then.

It is natural to crave relationships with others. It is natural to want to share relationships with those of whom you have common interests. It is natural in some of these cases to become attracted to these people. It is difficult however to discern this from a feeling that will make you think it is love. It is more likely that you have just 'fallen in love' and you will do this many times.

I've decided that's why it's called '*falling* in love.' After all if real love is a choice. Something you decide you will do, then you can't do it by accident. I chose to love my wife forever when I committed that love to her even before marriage. I have since always tried to show her this love through my actions. It is not accidental. It is done by thought process and through caring. It is many times natural and without effort because it has become simply part of who I am to love her. However, this as you can tell is not like falling in love.

When you fall in love you sort of just end up there. You sort of look around and say "How'd that happen?" It's a question of when

44

did I suddenly feel this connection become attraction? Or when did I suddenly feel a connection to this person of whom I feel attracted to and them to me? It's bumping into someone you've never met, but when you're eyes meet somehow you both feel that your souls have touched for at least an instant. You can love someone with all your heart and it won't change how you feel when things like this happen.

Just like I can put my hand in the freezer and when I touch a hot stove... well you get the idea.

We may be able to barricade our minds to some degree but barricading the feelings of our heart is not so easy.

I guess you could say love in some cases is choosing not to stay down every time you fall in love.

CHAPTER 8
Love is a gift.

I was having a fantastic conversation the other day. My wife and I were talking with two friends of ours, Abi and Mel, about love. The fact of love being a gift became a part of our conversation. This to me is in direct relationship to the opposing ideas of love being something you earn, love is something you have to work for or love is something you have to fight for. Let's talk for a second about what a gift is. First of all the next word that comes to mind following the word give or given is, away. I think that anything I have ever given away, I never expected it to be given back to me.

I think of being a child when you would occasionally give things that you knew eventually you would get something out of. For example, I got my sister a Star Wars board game for her birthday when in fact I was probably thinking just as much about getting to play it myself as I was about getting something for her. Other gifts have much more meaning and much better intention and even take a part of you.

For example, when I made my sister a necklace holder as a child, I was going to get nothing out of that at all. Instead it took up my time. I had to create it, using tools and materials and probably got a splinter along the way. The only thing I was going to get out of it was watching her enjoy it and being happy to have a place to hang up her necklaces. That's the thing a real gift should be and it should be given away without selfish intentions.

This begins to make me think how beautiful it would be if a relationship between two people looked like this. Two people always giving to one another. Giving each other time. Giving each other things. Giving each other actions of love. This might mean making the bed or doing the dishes. It might mean watching a ball game or dressing up or staying up late or going to bed early. There are all kinds of 'actions of love.'

Words are a gift. Saying I love you, thank you, honest words, helpful words, loving words. Sometimes an action of love is less visibly an action, just listening intently, not responding when someone is angry and instead giving them space. Think about your favorite gifts. Is that what you think of when you think of love?

Some of my favorite gifts are the ones I don't expect to get and always the ones that are personal where thought has been given to it. Not just something that was easy or took little effort but something that means the person knows me, really knows who I am. Not only do they know me but through the gift it shows that they accept that part of me and support me in who I am. Some gifts have been a surprise even when I asked for them. I am a huge Dallas Cowboys fan (I hope the portion of you who aren't or don't care will continue to read). Every Christmas and birthday it surprises me when I DON'T get an item with a star on it. I'm also a cyclist and I have so many cycling items that I can not use that are past gifts.

One Christmas, my wife got me several gifts I had wanted for years. I could have bought them but I wanted someone else to do it. Not because I couldn't or didn't want to do it myself but instead to show that they were willing to go above and beyond the easy gift. Plus, honestly like many gifts for special occasions they were those cool 'wants' I never bought for myself since they weren't things I needed.

I wanted my favorite English Cider, Strongbow. She went on line and ordered me 12. At the time it was very difficult to find in stores especially where we lived. I rationed those over the next year enjoying every one of them and with each one I thought about how she went to the effort to take the time to order these from an online store.

She also bought me a Park Bicycle Tool Pizza cutter. This was a big deal. She went to the bike shop in town where I shopped, told the owner about it and he ordered it. Sounds simple but yet no one I had known for years made this effort, including those whom I handed the catalog to and said, "I want this." Amazing, instead they just shot into the local department store and grabbed a Dallas Cowboys shirt. The latter gift means a person knows me but it doesn't mean they necessarily know me well. The earlier means a person knows me more deeply and is willing to connect with that part of me.

I, along with my wife, have been blessed to host many people in our home since we have married. This may seem like an inconvenience to many but it has truly been a never ending experience of growth, love and the meshing of lives beyond our own and those that are close to us. Diving in to life like one into water immersing one's self into it as if to say I am free from the captivity of land surrounded by what used to seem like the greatest wall ever built.

You see greater than the walls of the days of Rome or the Great Wall of China or the Berlin Wall, there is no political agreement that can be made to bring down the walls that hinder relationships. And if there are walls, I am boldly saying right now it is very difficult and possibly impossible that you will find a wide open, like a plane in the sky kind of love. You see, you hear people often talk about how someone in a relationship was not honest with them. That they put on a façade.

Chances are you and I have been that person whether with or without realization. Like a mime in an invisible box we allow people to see us on the outside, they see an expression painted on a face and we see them possibly in a similar way yet there is this big invisible box around both them and us. Now what, we try, like the mime, taking our hands, by our thoughts, up and down, feeling our way, but we can't seem to find a way out. Funny thing about these walls, these are invisible walls. They have no passageway, no key to a door and even if they did we most likely would not see it. Partially, because frankly as I already said, they are invisible.

The second and even more obviously analytical answer that no one likes to hear is that we don't want to. You'll often here me talk about the phrase, "I just don't know what to do". This HAS to be one of the most over used, unnecessary phrases in history. You've said it... yes you have and so have I. So has my wife, our parents, our siblings and every friend I can remember having any serious conversation with in regards to a struggle of any kind. Thing is many times we do know what to do; we simply choose not to do it. We choose denial because it is easier to be dumb than to be wise.

Want to hear something interesting? As I read 2 Peter 2: 20-21 I hear, "Better is the one who is ignorant than the one who knows but does not act on the wisdom given him." Mathew 25: 14-28 states that if a person does not use what is given to him he will not be given any more. Consider this with wisdom. It's as if God, in his parental type way is saying, "Why should I keep giving you knowledge when all you do with it is continue to respond, I don't know what to do!"

I wonder if God is ever baffled by those he's provided wisdom to make a decision that is painfully obvious and they still say this. Other things are generally clear. I know many persons who struggle with things like health, or doing well in school and it has nothing to do with a special condition or a lack of ability to learn. It has to do with one thing, discipline.

As a cyclist of more than 17 years, I have learned a great deal in regards to staying in shape, remaining healthy and general nutrition. I would get calls from people who tell me they just didn't know what to do about not losing weight and being in better shape. And let me just say, these are people I had know for years. I had seen what they were capable of and I knew their habits and so on. I knew they had cookies and candy all around the house and loved ice cream and others I knew had pizza at least once a week on top of their other lacking habits and none of them had any sort of exercise regimen at all. Now if they know that they had regular bad habits of eating, what they allowed in their home to eat and did no exercise, how is it they could say, "I just do not know what to do!"

Losing weight for a typical healthy person is simple. Eat fewer calories than you burn while eating balanced nutritious foods. To me this is like a smoker with a bad cough who doesn't understand why they have difficulty breathing! Now, I like most everyone struggle with self-discipline too. I have to follow the same things that I speak of and remind myself of what it is I know to be true.

The person who never studies can not wonder why they don't do well in school.

I am going to assume by now that I have made my point. I say this because in the back of my head I hear this voice saying, "Brad, you've made your point!"

So with that, I'd like to ask, "If you were to be given the wisdom, how would you use it? How have you used it in the past?"

Notes:

CHAPTER 9

Return to the façade...

Wisdom part 1:

You now have read that walls between people keep us from really knowing them. Not really knowing someone keeps you from loving someone because love is a choice and if either person is not real then one of the following occurs:

(A) The love is not real; it's just part of the show.

(B) You don't know who you love because they have a wall up.

(C) They don't know who they love because you have a wall up.

In the case of (B) and (C) eventually the walls always come down. This is why we here things like, "He wasn't who I thought he was." Exactly! When the walls come down and the real person comes out then the love escapes from that invisible box and it has to be re-created within the knowledge of reality and not that which is false.

I had a wonderful opportunity today to have coffee with a friend. A friend of whom I feel much closer to following our iced vanilla brewed coffee and caramel mocha blended iced coffee than I did before them. The amazing thing about this somewhat last minute get together fit between our tight schedules of work, auditions, and time pressed for other of life's priorities is that you can find love all over it!

Love was found in the first communication of effort to get together. It was found again by a quick response that showed respect of the other's invite and along with kind words expressing both interest and appreciation. Love appeared again when he contacted me with the slight open window he had in his schedule between commitments to get together and make note he had saw fit that this also fit in the window of availability I had given. Again showing respect, interest, and appreciation.

I'm not sure this new friend of mine realized how much this simple message of invitation based on past emails, texts, and social networking messages and of course I'm sure we had spoken at least once in the midst of hoping to meet, expressed love.

Love appeared in an effort to make a trip to the location of convenience and through all this we can see how much love is in a simple meeting between two persons looking to grab a cup of coffee, enjoy some good conversation and give it over to what may. I gained so much from the time we spent in this mid-town coffee shop. One in which I'm sure I had walked by and seen before but had never been to, via the invite, I was provided a new experience.

I learned this was a place in which persons in the arts utilize to gather and meet and discuss projects as well as their current life events. It looked like the usual chain coffee shop upon entering with the usual rhetoric and pace. However to the side was a stair way to a second floor. The décor resembled that of what you would expect in this place. It clearly had tables for greater seating as well as use for notepads and laptops so that groups from 2 -10 might be able to gather and develop the passion and ideas that engulfed their hearts and minds. It procured the air. You could sense it, that is if you left your space and allowed entrance in to theirs.

I did not have much time to do that myself. I was in a room of inspiration. I was in a room of excitement. Invisible walls had surrounded my friend and I as we spoke I saw the gleam in his eye and I sensed the same must have been seen in my own eye. We talked of our lives, of our friends, of our families, of our passions. We spoke of creating and from which I now created and have ideas noted to create even more.

Sharing is love. When one shares with you, note the honor in that. They could choose to tell anyone or no one. People will pay someone a great deal to listen to stories of joy and sorrow and experiences that sometime do not exactly fall into either category but a person still wishes to share.

Why are there so many late night infomercials, "He/She is only a call away…?" We crave intimacy in relationships. We crave sharing. Therapists are well paid to listen, noting this is only part of the work that they do of course. Even prostitutes have been interviewed and spoken about many clients who are not only looking for physical intimacy, but also an intimacy through conversation. In some cases for those who feel they have no one they can talk with or feel unable to talk they begin to use physical closeness to replace the inability to have deep, intimate personal conversations. To say that sharing in one another's lives is not loving when it is done in pure of heart and sincerity and that both persons are as interested in listening as they are talking, would be downplaying the beauty of such conversation as well as to dismiss one of the greatest actions of love that we have the ability to experience… if we should so choose.

I'm going to say this again and again so get used to it, love goes against the grain of what the greater world, society in general and the mediums of print, film and television would show you, except this print of course. Love forces us to think of someone else. Love says, "Do something for _____." (Fill in the blank) When asked about what we want, we are quick to think of things for ourselves. Love begins filling those thoughts with our hopes and dreams for others along side. The things that we begin to want are no longer tangible things like houses and cars and clothes but they are experiences with others that change lives. Both ours and theirs for the better.

Alright, so back to that iced vanilla coffee and blended iced coffee which by now is nearly empty. It's been a long time since I have been able to embrace a conversation with a friend such as this. My friend Gene and I had conversations like this when we both worked in radio years ago as did other friends and I of whom I had shared passions and interests. I had missed such conversation. I occasionally get to have these conversations by phone with friends who have gone on to fulfill their passions in places far away from here. While great, it's not the same.

True connection in any relationship is hindered when two people can not connect eye to eye. I think of those who are blind and how they touch something to see it. You can't do that over the phone. I can not imagine never holding my wife's hand for the first time. Or the embrace of a hug. And so I return, to our meeting. Before I walked in, I saw my friend already through the window. I saw him standing there in anticipation. Part of that was anticipation in what he was going to order, I saw him glancing toward the menu behind the baristas. However, I also saw him eagerly looking toward the door. As I walked in I saw him respond. First a little lean back, a smile, a raised eyebrow. Moving forward his hand outreached. Love. A firm hand shake, a question of how we were each doing and a thank you to and from each for getting together. Love. A move to order, a shared story and circumstance and we now return to where I had taken you just a page ago, the second floor.

As we engaged deeper into conversation we allowed each other deeper into one another's life. We learned about each other things we did not know, things we will remember for ever, things we will forget but will ask again because we want not to forget, but we want to hear and know so that it is engraved in our hearts as part of our friendship. We encouraged one other with our struggles and our successes. We laughed and we analyzed. Over two hours in a coffee shop we loved one another through engaging in shared interest of each others lives. It didn't fix anything or solve any great problem. It did provide fulfillment to a need we all have, the love of others and to love as well and know that love is a real thing.

I have provided these illustrations of love from this experience for several reasons.

My friend and I, while I would call him a friend are new friends, and this to me was truly the beginning of what I believe will be a great friendship. Key: New Friend

My friend and I are both straight men. Being able to talk about love outside of a romantic nature I believe is important. After all, love is not romance. Love is not just held between two people in such a way. Love can be found in may other places.

My friend and I had to work to make this little get together happen.

Other than a group activity we had passed hellos, and short, "Hey how's it going?" type talks along with a quick handshake and maybe the typical "guy hug" slap on the back but had not gotten together in the many months since we met and discussed the idea.

Notice also I don't believe either of us met or did any of these things because of obligation or emotion (feelings). No instead we did it by choice. We made the choice to love one another for simply the reason to give life a chance to happen to us. I'd like to thank my friend Vinny for showing me love.

Often I hear people say they don't see God. I also often hear people say they can't find love. I beg those persons out there who are saying this to re-read the story above. Do you see love now? Do you see the actions that represent love? Are you seeing that in your everyday life even if you don't see it every day? Are you making opportunities for such love to occur?

CHAPTER 10

Love your enemies.

Like love in any other circumstance in this one as well you must choose love. This may be the most difficult situation in which to love because you are loving that which you're insides tells you not only to not love but in many times you feel anger towards and sometimes even feelings nearing hatred. And so as I mention such feelings I remind again that feelings must derive from the actions of love and that you can not love with actions derived from emotional feelings.

You see once we begin to understand that love is an action a movement of our doing something we can begin to make choices of love, to love and regardless of the response continue to move in love. This is similar but not exactly like the idea of "killing them with kindness."

Allow me to step away for a moment to share an experience. When my wife and I moved to the New York area I had no idea I would experience anything I wasn't ready for. I had lived here before, I knew God had plans for us and I had been waiting to come back for six years. There were so many reasons I liked living in the area and still do enjoy all that it offers. One of those is the passion and drive of so many creative, talented persons. I so enjoy the energy and the pace of the people as well. However, there is something else I began to run into. Everyone is in competition also.

We have over 20 million people in this metropolitan area. And the very thing which can bond some of us can cause us to be willing to run right over each other. I have heard stories and personally seen people lie, cheat and steal to get on top in the smallest job, on Wall Street and in entertainment. Regardless of their background, be it poor or well to do, highly educated or not, there seems to be many in this world that are looking out to take advantage of whatever situation they can. I encountered this as well on some level in

Virginia but not like here, definitely in Oklahoma and Texas and for sure in Florida and California a great deal but the impact became more personal here and enemies were the result. By enemy I mean someone who looked at me as the one between them and what they wanted. At some point they held something against me and in some cases it would happen that I may have had something to hold against them.

I heard a message at a Church about praying for my enemies. Until now I never thought about them being my enemies but that was exactly the case. I didn't see it because I never considered myself part of the battle. Oh and let's not forget those who were battling me on the subway for a seat or the place with the most space.

There is the person who will walk a little faster to get ahead of you when going for a turnstile, a shot at being on the bus first, or the line to the pizza place or coffee shop. I do not believe there is any place where there is more competition other than right here in New York City.

I have often said driving in New York is like a giant video game and yes I consider myself to possibly be at the top of the list of names at the end with the high score. Competition for driving in New Jersey is a game of its own with its own rules. Pushing through gaps that barely exist and cutting across eight lanes toward the shortest toll line just to shoot back across eight lanes on the other side to get to your exit only a short distance away.

I say this with a purpose. You see you can not exist in a competitive environment without developing a natural set of enemies. Loving your enemies may mean giving up a seat and not fighting for it, it might mean taking the co-worker that is trying to cut you out so they can move up, a cup of coffee, it also most definitely means praying for them and being aware of a need which you may be able to meet. The other important thing to remember when you love your enemies is that you need to love yourself. You are not providing your self with love or being loving to yourself when you let anger fester toward others, when you remain bitter and move forward and away from whatever it is they did do or are doing to show the opposite of love. So treat yourself with love.

As scripture says in Philippians 4:4-9, "On whatever things are pure and good and holy concentrate on these things."

You see it is a matter of choice. Even in the case that your insides, your heart and your emotions may cringe when encountered with thoughts or a situation regarding an enemy you must choose to act different. Again, why, because you can not love or let the lack of loving be a derivative of feelings since love is not designed to follow in that way.

I get the feeling as I read this that if I was reading it for the first time as someone hurting in this situation that I'd respond with, "Ok, so that sounds good, but how?" So let me end this chaper with the following.

When you see that thing or hear that word or whatever it is that causes your insides to tighten up, stop and realize that person has needs and you have needs and while you may not be able to connect, that is ok. First, love yourself. It's very hard to give love if you don't have any love in you. For me that first means prayer to God. It second means that I must remind myself about some ways that I am blessed to have love from someone, even in those times where that someone may only be God himself. In which case, I remind myself that it is pretty cool that I can talk to the creator of the universe and know that he's listening and cares.

I might do something for myself. Many times I'll write down what I did. Then, I'll pray for that other person. I'll make recognition that they most likely have been hurt and/or are hurting from or by something. For both myself and them I remind myself that we are part of God's bigger story and I can not in any way foresee what he had in mind for us before, during, or following our experiences and interaction.

I do know we both need Him and we both need love and so I pray for love to be show to them as well and for their needs to be provided for. I pray for the waves of communication to open up.

Often enemies are created due to a lack of communication. I also pray for an understanding of one another since enemies are also often created from misunderstood differences.

Finally, if I believe I am to do something for them I look for a way to do it. I try to remain open to being able to see from their eyes. I figure if Jesus could come down to this earth to see as a man sees I can make the attempt to do the same for my fellow man, even those who oppose me.

CHAPTER 11

Love in definition... all of them

Love has many different appearances but like people, we may all look different but yet we're all the same in our design.

[*Love is not about a life mate.*]

In my favorite movie of all time: "American Flyers" we see two brothers. They are cyclists and are preparing for and competing in one of the biggest bike races in the United States. They lost their father years before to a Brain Aneurism and now one believes he has one; however unbeknownst to him it is actually his brother that has come down with this terminal ailment. The younger one whom is going to be ok looks at the older as he has now come to realize the truth and says something along the lines of, "I always swore I was going to say it, I love you too much for that." Sometimes Love requires sacrifice. Often the sacrifice is also a gift.

Also from "American Flyers" there is a kiss the day of stage two. It comes in light of the fact that the older brother is not doing so well and his friend and lover is sharing in this burden with him. She looks at him on an early morning with the sunrise coming through the window and they kiss. It is so sweet and passionate in the face of such turmoil. Instead of looking for passion when things are smooth and glossy look for it when things are rough not between you and another necessarily but in life. My wife and I for example have dealt with financial struggles, worries about being able to have children or for the lives of those in our family and the loss of them as well but we still have passion. In the movie Arthur, I remember after Arthur and Linda realize he is no longer rich, she being from a poorer class home says, "Let me show what we do to have fun when we can't afford to go out and begins to kiss him."

Being alone should be enough whether you are actually alone or alone with that special someone.

Is it possible to be in love yet not love? Is it possible to love but yet not be in love? Is what we call in love always love?

Here are some definitions of "love" as defined on Dictionary.com:

Pronunciation[luhv] Pronunciation Key - Show IPA Pronunciation noun, verb, loved, lov·ing. —noun

1   a profoundly tender, passionate affection for

another person.

I have this for people but does that mean I love them. Or is passionate affection truly the same as love? Think about it. Is that all you want love to be?

2   a feeling of warm personal attachment or

deep affection, as for a parent, child, or friend.

I feel personal attachment to people I know, even some whom I meet on the street yet truly do not know and it may be a feeling that is similar to that as for a friend but is that enough to say I love them?

3   sexual passion or desire.

Do I even have to go there? I, as many, have seen many persons whom I have desired in a sexual way. Does that alone mean I love them? After all, as a good friend of mine whom I was just talking to tonight said, "When a guy looks at me as I pass like this (head cranked around looking down as if toward her butt) I can't stand it, it's so disrespectful, I have a face!" If I were to tell her, it sounds like he loves you when he does this; I'm guessing she'd strongly disagree.

4   a person toward whom love is felt; beloved

person; sweetheart.

This is now defining a person. Huh? So a person to whom I have a sexual desire and feel attached to is actually love not those feelings. Now I'm really confused.

5   (used in direct address as a term of

endearment, affection, or the like): Would you

like to see a movie, love?

I'm ok with this. While it may not truly be a definition of the word in my mind, it definitely defines a common use of the word in a way that is not negative or in my mind out of line entirely. Though I have seen terms of endearment used loosely cause problems.

6   a love affair; an intensely amorous incident; amour.

I can't expand on this one as it is difficult to truly know what is meant. However, anything referred to as an incident seems hardly like what I would like to believe love truly is.

7   sexual intercourse; copulation.

Is this all love is? So anyone you have sex with you have loved? I *really* have a problem with this. Other wise, all many counties in Nevada have done is legalized 'love'.

8   (initial capital letter) a personification of sexual affection,

as Eros or Cupid.

(Same response as to #7)

9   affectionate concern for the well-being of others:

the love of one's neighbor.

Now this seems to me what love is. Her it is clear that affection means action. It is what Jesus referred to as Love. And wouldn't you want someone to have concern for your well being. Strangely enough, if you look out for someone's well being you may not use terms like "love" to them unless you feel it is appropriate. You may choose to *not* have sexual relations with them, yet you are sharing love.

10   strong predilection, enthusiasm, or liking

for anything: her love of books.

So if I feel enthusiasm toward something or liking for anything I love it. Would you want someone to say, I love you well, I have a strong liking and enthusiasm for you. It's the same thing, right?

11   the benevolent affection of God for His creatures,

or the reverent affection due from them to God.

This greatly depends on your view of the word affection. In most of my reading, it is read as an action and not a feeling. This seems fitting for describing love only in that case. Affection is similar to love in definition by most of our world anyhow. After all we talk about feeling or having affection for someone. In fact affection should be evident by something we show or do. For example, I show her affection by running my fingers through her hair.

12   Chiefly Tennis. a score of zero; nothing.
        (Sports fans?)

13   a word formerly used in communications to represent
        the letter L. verb (used with object)
        (Covered this)

14   to have love or affection for: All her pupils love her.
        (Covered this)

15   to have a profoundly tender, passionate affection for
        (another person).
        (Covered this)

16   to have a strong liking for; take great pleasure in:
        to love music.
        (Covered this)

17   to need or require; benefit greatly from: Plants love sunlight.

Hmmm, I've never thought about loving something being a need
or requirement. I believe this is like saying I love food. I don't say
it because I need or require so much as the fact that I really enjoy
it or have a longing for it. I.e.: I love Steak. Saying Plants love
sunlight only works for plants that respond well to lots of sun.
Some plants respond well when living in more shaded areas. So
what is better defined is the 2nd half that says to benefit greatly
from. So is that how you want someone to love you, selfishly. I
love you because I need or require you to exist. Or how about, I
love you because it benefits me, I get something out of it. So I
don't love you because I want to but because it is good for me or

because I have to. That does not sound like the kind of love me
or many people I know are looking for.

18   to embrace and kiss (someone), as a lover.

        This is a physical action. I could kiss a random person
        on the street and I'm pretty confident that doesn't mean it's love.

19   to have sexual intercourse with.

        –verb (used without object) Brothels house love?
        I don't think so.

20   to have love or affection for another person; be in love.

        —Verb phrase   And this is where I'm going.
        It says here to have love is love. My question is,
        should it be that when we love, we then have love?
        Yet, it isn't always the other way around. What is affection?
        Is it an action or a feeling?

21   love up, to hug and cuddle: She loves him up every
        chance she gets.
        —Idioms I won't comment on this one since
        I've never really heard this used.

a   out of affection or liking; for pleasure.

        without compensation; gratuitously: He

b   took care of the poor for love.

A and B are completely in opposition. A. talks about love being selfishly done and B. talks about it being unselfish. Which love do you give others? Which one do you want to receive? Are your answers to these two questions in contradiction to one another?

Notes:

23   for the love of, in consideration of; for the sake of:

        For the love of mercy, stop that noise.

Not a definition of the word love but definitely a way I've used it!

24   in love, infused with or feeling deep affection or passion:

        a youth always in love.

25   in love with, feeling deep affection or passion for

        (a person, idea, occupation, etc.); enamored of:

        in love with the girl next door; in love with one's work.

Notice that these are definitions more of the phrase "in love" than it is of the word love it self. To be in love, is to be infused with or feeling.... In another words this is more about a feeling than the action or verb of moving with love.

26   Make Love

    a   to embrace and kiss as lovers.

    b   to engage in sexual activity.

I guess I could go back to mentioning Nevada again. Instead though, I will say, have you ever know someone, maybe yourself that has embraced, kissed or even engaged in sexual activity with someone who they did not 'love' truly. Would you consider what happens when the boss has an affair with his secretary type story to be love? What about when the lady engages in such actions in order to get something from a man, is that love?

27   no love lost, dislike; animosity: There was

        no love lost between the two brothers.

This is a reverse of love so we are skipping right over it. Maybe I'll make that the sequel to this book.

As you can see these are very poor definitions alone of the word love as it is by itself and its meaning. Even though they may be fitting, they either are scary, sad or at the least in many cases NOT what we want when we think of the word. At least not in, and of themselves. Let's look at some of the positive ones. Please go back and pick out the ones that explain how you would want someone to love you.

Notes:

1-5 are all wonderful but alone none of them are all that I would want from the love of someone.

9 is the perfect definition of the kind of love I would want. The actions that we are instructed to give when how to love as we read in the Bible, to love others, treats it like an action. It says we should do something, that we should make an action. Follow that with the way God loves us. It may not always be easy and it may not always mean that we get something back but it is still something we do. Why, that's the interesting thing, there is no why. These types of love don't always give you something back. They are not selfish. You simply <u>do</u> this kind of love.

Now imagine 9 combined with 1-5 and as well combined with 14-16, 18-20, 22b, 24, 25 and 26. In my humble opinion to love with any of these and not include 9 then they begin to seem very empty and passing. They seem to be more of an activity that passes us by than that of something on going that is given, received and shared as we would want it from others.

Think about the actions you believe show love. Think about how it is referred to when you hear about how God so loved the world that he... And that Jesus said to love God with or to love others as... Always clearly it is used as an action. Men love your wives as... Women love your husbands as.... Etc...

And so based on the definitions we read above and the history of the word, love can be used in so many ways. However, love as we are talking about in this book is that of an action and an attitude, a way. It is not about affection alone. It is not about simply feeling a strong liking for someone. It is not just a physical embrace or sexual act. It is definitely not doing something for your own benefit or simply for survival. So what is it?

As we continue to explore this word love, we look at it as we would want it to be, an action. A way of being that is ongoing. It includes actions mentioned above but done in a way that is for the benefit of others even if it happens to benefit one's self also. It may bring a feeling or a feeling may precede the action however the action it self is not done or controlled solely from said feelings. The love we speak of that we are all so intensely searching for and anxiously awaiting to find is that of one that is not like the way I love to write or love to bike ride or even to love as I love the Dallas Cowboys. Granted, those around me might want me to love them as passionately as all those things. But when the Cowboys play badly I yell and scream.

When I can't ride I simply put the bike aside and have no interaction until it benefits me and I can make time for it and if I don't feel like writing I don't. I believe you will agree that is not how any of us want to be loved. Instead however we want to be loved passionately and with enthusiasm and with every part of one's being, not as I do with all 3 of the aforementioned loves as I decide I want to and I can and I choose to at my convenience.

The key there is we want them, when we need them, and we want such love because another person chooses to do so and we want it to be ongoing not just when someone can make a little room to fit it into their lives.

I realize that from here on out we should make love for any "thing" or person we simply have an affection toward with a lower case l. This little l, is how I love my bike, my Dallas Cowboys and my opportunities to sit in the coffee shop or park which is something I love to do and write. It is with the little l that I think we talk when we say I'm in love with him/her and our eyes get big and glassy and we can see nothing but excitement in the glow of a new relationship or maybe even an old one.

However, for those we are striving to love continuously in such a way that is clear and seen by our actions that we hope to always be unselfish for their benefit. For this to be given, received and shared in such a way between them and us we will use an upper case L.

CHAPTER 12

Scheduling Love

You have probably heard the phrase that "we choose whether or not to be happy. In choosing not to be happy we are choosing to be unhappy." I completely believe this though, I may not like it. I especially don't like it when I'm unhappy with something in my life because I know in many/most cases I could probably just turn that frown upside down and do something to make it better. However, it always means overcoming something I feel with doing something, an action of Love for myself.

It may sound funny but we are willing to make sure we get to do the things we love the most, many times we schedule them aside. I could talk about your favorite TV show, football on Sunday afternoons, as a kid it was Saturday morning cartoons. I have always set aside specific times through out the week and on the weekends to ride my bike. As an avid cyclist this has a plays an important role in my feeling good and being happy with how I'm living my life.

When I don't do this I mope about it. Sometimes I find a way to make it happen even if it's not in the way I'd prefer. Maybe I have to ride at night instead of in the morning. This may mean riding an indoor trainer rather than outside. Still, I'd rather get to ride some than not at all, so when I stop complaining about not getting to ride, and then stop complaining about how I'm unable to ride when and how I want, I just simply get on the bike anyway I can and the joy of the ride ensues at least on some level and I feel better than had I not ridden at all and concentrated on the "I can't..."

Sometimes, Love is like this. Sure we want Love to be spontaneous. We want him or her to know just what I want and to know just when I want it and just how to give it and hopefully sometimes he/she will. Other times however he or she just needs to be told. So lose your pride and make way for the one you're with to Love you. On the flipside, we have to be willing to Love others as they need to be loved. If snuggling up with someone for their favorite shows on Tuesday night is a scheduled opportunity to show Love then do it. If you're married and have kids and are losing time, then schedule a Date Night. At the time I write this section, my wife and I don't have kids yet and still due to our busy schedules we have considered doing this.

My point is just because something is scheduled or done in a way not quite how you'd choose, many times still doing what you love will create joy and put a smile on your face. So, don't be afraid to schedule times for Love to happen now and then. Actually this is one of the things I like about going to Church on Sunday's now. I was never much of a Churchgoer before, however, now I am.

I've always wanted to know God more and have made efforts to search Him out. However; now I know I will get to spend at least a couple very personal hours with Him each week. I still try to take time to study and pray when I can through the week. Yet, Church becomes like that one on one time you get hanging with the one you love at a coffee shop or maybe talking on a road trip. Not only have Sunday's not become mundane due their scheduling, I look more forward to Sundays now than ever because I'm looking forward to our time together. So, again I say, don't be afraid to schedule Love. On a side note, you still want to be spontaneous now and then. It's just fun!

CHAPTER 13

Seasons and Feelings - Both change so be careful

As we talk about feelings and emotions controlling us I'd like to make the comparison to the seasons. As seasons pass, at least in most places, you have hot days in the summer and cold days in the winter. You can't change that. You can't make it 90 degrees on a cold winter's day and you can't make it snow in summertime. (I just had a flashback of The Year without a Santa Claus) The fact is in Southwest Texas in July and August it is going to be hot, very, very hot. In Buffalo in January it's going to be cold, very, very cold. Now let's take a look at this. I love the winters but even I have my limit. I like the cold crisp air and I enjoy snow like I'm still 7 years old. I still break out a sleigh and go find a big hill when the opportunity arises and I wish for that opportunity each year.

However, I also can find enjoyment in the summer; this is when I get to do the majority of my cycling. I have to tell you though a lot of those summer days when it's creeping around 100 degrees you can really not want to be on the bike, kinda like those 30 degree days in the winter. I love cycling. I've never been one who let temperatures determine whether I ride. I've ridden in rain, cold, heat, when I've felt great, when I've felt, well, not so great. Imagine if we Loved others this same way. Regardless of how we 'felt' if we still made the effort to enjoy them, to help them enjoy life to share joy with them in a way that meant, it's not about how I feel or if my emotions are there it's about you and me. Me choosing to Love you because I can't imagine not or better yet I actually enjoy Loving you.

We then make choices every day because it is simply the best decision and not simply because we feel like it. I might be able to dress a certain way in a controlled temperature and look in the mirror and feel good about myself however, that doesn't mean I should really go out that way.

Let's imagine for a second if we said I don't care if it's cold, I'm not wearing winter clothes and I'm going to go do _____, I'm wearing my favorite t-shirt and shorts. Well, typically you end up sick. And what about in the summer? I love winter clothes but you will not find me in a turtle neck and a coat unless it's below freezing. On a hot summer day it would probably kill me.

Don't be afraid to look past what feels good now to choose what's best. Generally then, you look back happier than had you made the choices based on the feelings you had looking forward.

If you're reading this, you have an interest in something different than what you have known as love for so long. You probably don't like what love has felt like. Maybe someone said they loved you and they hurt you and now you question love altogether and I can't say that I blame you if that's the case. Whatever the reason is that you picked up this book, I hope, you, unlike so many are willing to think different, to see something new with an old set of eyes. If so, then I'd say you're the few and not the many. That's one of the crazy things I'll never understand is how few people I encounter want something different than that which hurts them, or doesn't work for them.

Funny you would not continue to eat at a place that had bad service and served bad food and that was dirty. Well, would you? You would not continue to go out to a car each morning, before time to go to work, that you knew for a fact was so broken down that it was never going to start. You would not continue to go outside and sit in it and try to start it again and again every day. Well, would you? Would you do either of these over and over and every time simply get more angry and more angry? Would you? If you said you would, then I hope you'll consider the idea of finding someplace new to eat and getting a bus pass, cause things do not change without some sort of effort put into them.

On that note, many times things are fine and it is in us that we find the problem. I love ambiance, I love good service, and I really love a well made coffee. I'm talking the kind of coffee that a person puts their heart into making. The blend is fresh. The syrups aren't straight in but are melted in along with the pouring of the milk. And the whip cream, well, the whip cream is home made and topped with your favorite topping too. I'll admit it. As I sit in a 'chain' coffee shop I'm not nearly enjoying myself the same way I am as when I go to my favorite little West Village coffee shop. What I mentioned a moment ago is what I'd have gotten there. Here, the people were very nice. The chairs aren't so comfortable, the space is a bit tight, and it's noisier than most. The only art on the wall is to promote the coffee they sell, not support the local artist. The coffee, well, the coffee is, let's just assume you've gotten my point.

I'll be honest again. My favorite coffee shop doesn't serve the very best coffee. It is however in a quaint little place off the beaten path where you'll walk in off of the cobblestone roads, not a busy street with bustling cabs. The art on the wall is wonderfully captivating and does support someone who painted them with their heart and hands. It's quiet and there are couches. Sure the regular chairs are only slightly better than these. However, they feel better when you see the art on the wall. The large chalk boards behind the barista's add to the feel too. The many, many options hand written and at any time they might squeeze in a fresh and fun, new idea in yet another color. Cinnamon sticks may not make the coffee that much better than it is here, yet, having them there, and taking one and placing it in your mug is oh so pleasing. Yes, a mug. When is the last time if ever that this place used mugs instead of large paper cups. And anyone will tell you presentation is everything.

This is why we say a first impression is so important. How we perceive things effect what we think of it, whether we like it or not. I say this because the coffee could be better here than my favorite spot for java and I would still go there. The people may not be as pleasant but I still go there. You see it's a place that takes me away, not just a place to get a cup of coffee. My point is sometimes we can get the same thing from two places and it's going to be exactly the same. It's up to us to recognize that we're making the choice of one over the other for aesthetically pleasing reasons.

CHAPTER 14

Want to change your emotions? Change your actions.

I often tell people you have to change the way you think in order to live based on the truth of words such as love. Many people I have spoken to ask me, "If you can show me how to change how I think I'll be happy to do so." My answer for them is this, "Want to change your emotions? Change your actions." Generally, as we've discussed we allow our emotions to determine our choices when we are typically much better off making good choices and seeing the emotions that develop from those choices are truly good as well. Again, it is similar to what I have brought up about instant gratification. Emotionally I may want to go do this or that right now and it might feel good right away however the outcome, the result of the decision based on those emotions might come back to hurt me later.

I know many couples who have discussed whether it is ok to go out with others they know of the opposite sex. In many cases, it may not be a negative impact at all. However, in several cases, a person get's excited about the idea of going out, then they get excited about going out with a certain person that they enjoy the time of. If that person is of the opposite sex there is a risk that that emotion of excitement coupled with the environment they go into (for example the local watering hole) added with a connection of interests could cause more feelings to arise. This is how people are torn apart by what appears to be mere friendships. You see, emotions can be quite dangerous. But what if you thought to yourself, the best decision is for me to go home to my spouse. And, if I feel a need to go out, then I will take him/her out when I get home to our favorite spot, or plan to go out on a night we can be together. Another option might be to call your significant other to join you to go with this other person and as well invite others from work, or the mutual hobby interest, along as well. A group environment usually helps you keep these emotions in check and you can redirect your excitement and focus on the one you have a commitment to rather than risk developing confusing emotions for another person by being out with them alone.

This is a simple matter of changing how you think and what you think is loving, what you think is the choices that give life, what is freedom and so forth.

Love trumps fear—

Are you afraid of Love? Are you afraid of what might happen if you do? Love trumps fear. True Love overcomes the fears that often get in the way of our ability to have life and live it to the fullest. You might be saying, I'm not afraid to Love, I'm afraid of being hurt. It is the same. You may say, I'm only afraid of what getting into a relationship will cause me to lose, then that to is the same. Most, I believe do not want to Love truly. They want to love with their rules. These are the rules of most love stories and romance novels and movies and television shows. Like so many things we want to take ideas that sound good and make them better by spinning them to work our way. Our way says, I can love someone and still spend a lot of free time with the friend whom I have a connection with and never let it get in the way. Until, we aren't spending much time with the person we so call love at all. Then we don't understand why we feel disconnected.

True Love makes a different decision; true Love helps us overcome the fear of reducing our time in those other relationships or taking a different approach to having them. It does not say you can't, it says you can if you'll do it like this and you can have Love too. You can Love both persons and Love them fully and achieve a development of these relationships more completely and for life when you Love as Love was meant to be, by our choices. Maybe you're afraid you will get hurt. Instead do not be afraid to gain all that you can when you receive and give Love. We risk being hurt in every choice we make. I have risked being hurt by not being willing to Love as well. I have chosen to not show love when I was angry with someone. Rather than confront them and develop a resolution and at least provide an opportunity for Love to be exchanged and for the life giving emotions to occur I ignored them. I did not call them or

speak with them. What happened during those months? Did I gain anything? Is it possible I was more hurt by not having this person in my life than if I had? I'll never know. Again, this was someone whom I knew very well. Much later in life we began to be more honest when we felt hurt or confused by one another's actions. Suddenly we were truly Loving each other. Suddenly we began to get closer, more comfortable with being real and it developed parts of who we are that we had not yet explored. Our relationship grew out of this time together even when it came from one of us hurting the other because we became willing to make right choices even in the midst of some very strong and difficult emotions saying not to. In these cases the choices to Love ourselves and each other allowed us to bring life to ourselves and one another. I even believe this spilled over into other relationships. After all, as we read before…
He who heeds discipline shows the way of life.

Hold Me! And Give me space! – At the same time…

A close friend of mine was recently in only his second serious relationship. In his 20's he and an old friend had begun to rekindle a relationship and it was developing into much more than friends. He was working hard to see if it was emotions from a choice to love or if these feelings were causing the choices. I could see however, he was beginning to work, too hard. You know how this is. (for this case I'm referring to he and she but this is a personality trait issue and can honestly go either way) She was nervous about the situation. She needed some space. He was excited about what the relationship had in store and wanted to know what she was thinking and feeling. He, having had few serious relationships needed regular reassurance that everything was going to be ok. He was afraid. I became concerned when I realized he would not let things work out as each person needed them to. Instead, he would press wanting to call, to ask her if she was alright, ask if he could do anything to help, etc. You see in his mind, he was, loving her. However, loving her, in a way that Love would "trump his fears" would have been to say, I'm here, I Love you, by letting her call and still calling and showing confidence and faith that Love would prevail.

Does this mean they would end up together? No. It means that his confidence is that what is right, what will bring life, will happen. You see, the biggest fear is when we look back knowing we did not do things 'the right/best way' and we have to ask, "What if…" Instead be able to have done all you can. Love a person where they are, and put yourself in a place to be Loved where you are at. If we have communicated what we need and know what they need. If we put the greatest need in front. If we do this and choose Love first regardless of all the feelings and emotions that often get in the way then we can trust Love to prevail. If that love is derived from actions that create a friendship, a long term relationship and marriage or whatever might come, we can know it came from True Love, not simply a series of emotions and feelings and from those reactions from fear, anxiousness, excitement, lust and so forth. Then we never have to look back and think what if I had not acted out of lust? What if I had not acted out of fear? What if I had not come on so strong and pushed so hard in reaction to my anxiousness and excitement? What if I had asked myself, what do they need, how will they feel loved, what is the action that will most show love and respond with the answer provided. Then and only then can you give a person space and hold them at the same time where they are and when it is needed rather than out of selfish desires, wants, and concerns and instead out of Love in the truest meaning of the word.

You see I told my friend you care too much and that is not loving. You are not giving her any space and that is not loving. You must show her how much you care by giving her space and showing confidence by not caring so much. Your constant efforts to handle things, to care to understand are not allowing for any space for her to develop thoughts and provide you with the very answers you so badly are seeking. Instead by providing space, showing confidence you inspire confidence, you allow for a person to develop and in return show you who they are. You get the answers that you need.

(Story time)

When my wife and I first met we had just shortly before been in very serious relationships. (Now we have had our 5th anniversary with the 6th only four months away.) We had been in relationships that had caused a lot of trauma, fear, and so forth. Personally, I told her, I had A.D. This was my acronym for a disease that I had come up with, Association Disorder.

"Love allows room for our shortcomings and yet holds us accountable to be better. The response of love to this is seeing an area as not good in our life, appreciating those who loved us enough to give us grace in those times no matter how short lived they are and do the same for them."

A.D. quickly became our code for, "I'm not over this yet, I'm still working on something connected to that thing, whether it be as simple as a word, phrase, TV show, movie, car, town (city) or whatever." It basically said, in short, "I need space for that." Lisa used this on occasion, I used it often! I am a very emotional, hold on to the bitter end, struggle with letting go, giving grace forgiving kind of guy, no matter how hard I try to be otherwise. If it is big and bad enough my wife can and has been the same, so she tells me. I've been blessed to see her mercy and grace much more than if not always over this other side. Here's the key, you can't keep having A.D. forever. A.D. should be like a headache, the flu or the common cold. They enter your life and cause pain but you know or should trust in the fact that these ailments will go away. They are rarely and generally are not life threatening. If you address them properly, with lots of fluids rest, chicken soup and some common medicines they will go away. What you aren't guaranteed is for how short or long they will last. Still, the pain should fade and eventually go away.

Does that mean you don't connect them? No, like we may remember the pain of our last cold or maybe even what caused it. I always associate sleeping with windows open during a change of season with getting the sniffles which usually turns to a cold and occasionally a flu that feels like an overly intense case of bad allergies combined. However, it's not 100% that I always get it when I sleep with the windows open during the change of seasons. In the same way we tend to keep some association and memory of these pains without actually feeling the pain the next time we hear about this or come across that thing.

"The key to A.D. is to strengthen not weaken love"

The key to this whole A.D. story isn't recognizing the A.D., while this is important. It is not either simply enough that we allow one another to recognize and deal with the A.D., though without this the key point could never come to fruition. The key is that we fulfill our part, when we are confronted with the A.D. continue to work to accept any responsibility involved, realize the fact that it is exactly just what we call it. A: Association, it is not the problem, it can not hurt us. We simply are associating it with a problem or something that used to cause us pain but it itself can no longer hurt us unless we continue to allow it. This leads us to D: Disorder. To quote one of my favorite movies, Stripes, where several men join the army, most older and out of shape than the average army recruit, but each are trying to prove something to themselves in doing so… "Something is wrong with us, something is very, very wrong with us!"

The question is are we going to take on the challenge, are we going to do what we came into this new relationship to do, to overcome, to move forward, to fulfill a Love that is beyond our imagination with the experience of whatever pains and joys of our past we have, or are we going to say, I can't, I'm too old, too beaten up to accomplish this and just continue to focus on those areas of association. Are we going to let ourselves get beat by something as simple as the common cold? You see, like the common cold there's no cure. A cure implies that it can be treated and will never return. As long as we make ourselves vulnerable, as long as we are willing to Love we can be impacted by a sort of A.D. However, the key is facing those issues, embracing them, knowing they aren't going to disappear entirely and yet know that the pain of them, the disorder of the association, will go away if we press forward. I like to complete this process by sharing what it was with the person I'm with, or at the very least, know that they realize I'm not saying A.D. so much any more. This let's each person know, I've dealt with this, your Love allowed me to overcome it by your allowing space. Then mercy and grace entered the situation and became part of the healing. Thank you. Your Love, allowed me to heal, to grow, to Love and return and vice versa. That is the key.

'It is as loving to take responsibility as it is to show Love through respect to those who do this.

Thank you for this, not, that's right you better feel that way.'

>>>*I just went out to eat. I've been to this restaurant twice in my life. Both times the location was decided by friends. I could have eaten somewhere else however, it would have meant not spending precious time with my dear friends. The food is not really so good, but it's amazing how much I enjoyed it. Again, the point is that I chose to enjoy it and not just keep comparing it to the place up the road that I like so much more. My question to you is what are you choosing? It is our choices that lead us to love. It is our choices that prove our love. Love you see, is a choice.*<<<

CHAPTER 15

Love is a choice, period

Love is a choice of action. This action can mean it is something we do as well as an action of allowing someone else to 'not love' in their human frailty. You see, we aren't going to Love anyone or anything perfectly all the time. I'd love to say I Love my wife as I should and as I wish to all the time. While this is truly my goal, there are times when I am selfish, there are times when I act without thinking of how this will affect her, or maybe I even think of it yet my love of my own self and my interest for what I want right in that moment wins over my Love for her. Yet, her actions of grace in letting me act out in whatever way I may have and still standing by my side is truly one of the biggest actions of Love.

My understanding that my choice not to Love her in a moment, is like my slipping on my attempts to eat healthy 100%. A slight over-indulgence and lack of discipline, giving into what I know is right and caring more for that which my emotions and weaknesses cry out for so much that I simply give in and act. There goes the whole tub of ice cream when a cup would have done fine.

A cup now and then is fine it would not negate the exercise and the salads and the eating vegetables but a whole tub. I always regret eating that whole tub too. It makes me feel quite sick. I'm usually pretty down on myself following my actions. Shaking my head, I wonder why I did such a thing. If I really cared anything at all about myself I'd have either not had any at all or had enough self discipline to have only had a cup instead of going after the whole tub with a big spoon and a bag of Oreos. Oh, I didn't mention the Oreos did I?

You see, it's those times we might see that we're being selfish and doing something for us over the one we 'love.' Usually, however, the things we're choosing to do aren't even Love for ourselves.

He who heeds discipline shows the way of life, but whoever ignores correction leads others astray.

Proverbs 10:17

You see Love is a choice, therefore a discipline. We may not like that as I think we find discipline to be a confining word. However, do you find more freedom in having what you want immediately or being able to be what you want long term? These often do not connect. I want to live to be a 100. I really do, if not longer. I want a very long healthy life. I want to still be riding my bike, possibly even racing into my 70's and 80's. I really do. How I eat, drink and in general choose to take care of my body when an opportunity for instant gratification arises will much determine my long term happiness and therefore my long term freedom. I do not want to be in a situation in 20 years where I can not toss a football with the son I hope to have, or still go for long walks with the daughter that is on her way into this world.

You see our view on freedom, once corrected can then affect our view on discipline, choices, and from that new vantage point we can best view how to love ourselves and others. You see, the second half of Proverbs 10:17 clearly states that those who ignore correction, who do not heed discipline leads others astray. I often will do fine avoiding things that are bad for me unless I'm around those who say, "Eh, what's just one." or "Well, it might not be good for you but I'm going to have some." These things may not always be bad in moderation however; in some cases they may not be good at all. Their damaging potential to me is much, and I should be more concerned with that than the instant gratification. Again, our view on the areas mentioned above, freedom, discipline and Love will determine our actions for ourselves and others.

On that note, let me say we do have to Love ourselves, truly take care of ourselves before we can ever Love and care for anyone else. This is also something to watch out for when you see others.

How do they care for themselves? Do they take care of themselves and make good choices for themselves? Do they know themselves well? Do they make the best choices for themselves?

If not then why may I ask do you think they would make the best choices for you? And notice when I ask how they treat themselves I'm not asking if they spoil themselves with indulgences. This is a two fold danger, meaning either they could turn out to be selfish and continue to do this and be too into their selves to care about your wants or they'll do as much or more for you and neither means Love. Love can be tough. I don't buy coffee at a coffee shop every day, because of Love. I Love my wife, us and myself and I want to pay off our credit cards. Love is a choice. Many times we come upon Love at a crossroads and you have to look at the signs and choose the road that will lead you to where you want to go. Sometimes the road to Love is long and takes you through the desert.

Notes:

Changing our definition

CHAPTER 16

Walking in the Desert

I'm not sure why we always tend to think that a walk in the desert is so bad. Actually, I do, I mean after all, what do you think of when you think of the desert? I'd guess most people would say hot, lonely, hard, nothingness, sandy, and many other words that combine to define a very sad and barren place. We also tend to associate the word lost with the desert. Really, when you think about it, the desert is just a beach with no ocean. One of my favorite beaches is Jones Beach in Long Island, NY. My wife likes the water there but is not so fond of that particular beach.

Don't misunderstand me, she doesn't mind the sand and she appreciates that there's plenty of room for everyone however there would be enough room for everyone even if they each brought 5 more friends, maybe 10! The beach is HUGE. This means from the very nice parking lot, through the very nice pavilion / changing area onto the very nice sand that goes on and on and well, on. To me it's entirely worth it. It's a wide open soft sandy beach with clean water near New York City and it is worth crossing, what to some could seem like a desert.

I wonder, what if we thought of the desert more like we think of the red carpet. The carpet itself is really an amazing place isn't it? Have you ever seen celebrities 'walk the red carpet?' You can tell from the moment they exit their car and the safety it provides that they have to prepare themselves for the public battle they are about to embrace. If you have never experienced this, allow me to walk you through it. They step foot onto the carpet and immediately eyes of all kinds turn their way. There are eyes that envy, the eyes who stare in awe, the eyes looking for a photo to bring a paycheck, eyes looking for a flaw. They see the eyes of those who follow each red carpet walk, looking for the autograph they don't yet have the eyes of those with a microphone in hand and behind those are the eyes of a cameraman.

Can you imagine all the eyes looking at you? Now imagine the expectation. Expected to be beautiful and look 10 years younger than you are old or in some cases 10 years more than you really are, if you are too young for the older fan but trying to break from the younger ones as well. Expectations that you'll be dressed the very best although that also will be expected of all the rest. Each one to step on the red carpet is compared by the eyes of those that stare. Still there is more and from this point forward everyone begins to yell their name.

Everyone, all these eyes now turning into hands reaching out want to be recognized, just acknowledged by them. They have the weight of all those who believe they could change their lives with a word or the touch of a hand. All of the reporters who want an interview, just an answer to a few questions, the flash of a hundred cameras going off again and again. They can't stop smiling, they must continue to make their way and be polite and wonderful to everyone.

What a relief it must be to get to the end of the red carpet and if they win the award or the premier is a success it must make the memory of the red carpet a little sweeter a little less stressful maybe even they look back and wish they would have spent a little more time on that carpet, taken a few more photos, signed a few more autographs, and answered a few more questions. My thought is this, Jesus walked the desert tempted by the Devil for 40 days before he began His ministry but His ministry became one that has stood the test of over 2000 years.

If we're willing to walk the desert in appreciation, if we are willing to look at what we can take from being in the desert, if we can even stop to see what we are supposed to leave in the desert then possibly when we get to the other side, it'll be a beautiful ocean, an award from showing success, or a ministry that touches the lives of many. And if it is, how much better will we be able to look back at that walk in the desert? How different will we be? I'm not saying to change what you believe the desert to be when you are in it, I'm saying maybe you, and I for that matter, should change who we are when we are in the desert. Why did I just spend 2 pages talking about a walk in the desert? Because those I know who Love the greatest have crossed some very long deserts before being able to do so.

Those from that group who treated the desert like a red carpet believing there was something great on the other side not only Love others greatly but Love life greatly and appreciate this Love. They also see God's Love, which is far vaster than the desert and the ocean combined. And so, they Love like they never could have ever loved before their foot stepped into that hot, hot sand. Let me just add this. Sometimes, we have to remember, the sand comes to us when we're just in the midst of walking, keep walking if you see the desert surround you. Walk in the right path that only His Love in your heart can lead you. Embrace it. It's part of the journey.

When you walk through the desert with the one you Love then you'll find this to be twice as true. It's an opportunity to bond and strengthen much more than you would have alone or had you fallen in the heat. I hope you will choose to carry one another and embrace the walk together.

The desert is a lot like training for an athlete. I've heard that Mohammed Ali once said, "I hated every moment of training, but I loved to fight."

Many athletes I know love the training even when it's really hard. I love to ride my bike. I used to hate climbing, and when I'm out of shape I still do. Even when I'm in shape I'm an awful climber compared to most of my peer cyclists. Yet, when I'm riding and training on a regular basis there's something I find glorious about the climb, to conquer a hill or a mountain. To ride with a fluid spin of the pedals like the greats who've ridden the Alps in France.

Still, I think of what Mohammed Ali said and I think, if I hated training, I'm not so sure I'd ever do it just to race. Of course, I'm not as good of a cyclist as he was a fighter, but still. Can you imagine doing anything that requires so much of your time that you absolutely can't stand just to on a very rare occasion get to do something you really enjoy, to do that one thing now and then that gives you the greatest natural high there is? I can't yet he did. It resonates with me more now.

I hate walking in the desert but I love getting to the other side. I don't like climbing the mountain. I like getting to the top and knowing I've conquered it. I don't like confronting the hard things in my relationship, but I love seeing the result of when my wife and I grow from the honesty. I may not like walking the red carpet and having to get my feet callused in the hot sand but I love getting to the other side and jumping in the beautiful water and soaking up the sun.

Ali's statement helps me to remember that we should embrace the difficult things that make us strong enough to beat our ultimate opponent when it counts.

In scripture Paul says, "I don't do what I want, I do what I don't want" and then he adds, "Lord, why have you put this thorn in my side?"

I believe it's true that he didn't like that thorn that caused him to struggle but maybe that is what reminded him of God's Love and kept him turning to that Love. Maybe the pain of that thorn kept him from enduring the pain of losing to the ultimate opponent. Keep up the good fight, racing the race set before us, even when it means training hard, climbing mountains and crossing deserts.

This will surely allow our Love to be seen and for us to be known by it. Training shows we're serious. Ali would have never gotten his first chance to fight without training. For that matter he might never have been taken seriously had it not been for his training. You don't have to like it. You do however have to endure the training to enjoy the victory.

Famous Words

The most famous words about Love: Love is patient, Love is kind. It does not envy, it does not boast, it is not proud. It is not rude, it is not self-seeking, it is not easily angered, it keeps no record of wrongs. Love does not delight in evil but rejoices with the truth. It always protects, always trusts, always hopes, always perseveres. Love never fails. (though we sometimes fail to Love).

These famous words about Love should sound very familiar. They are from 1 Corinthians 13: 4-8. By now you've heard some or all of them in at least eleven Sermons, five weddings, three offerings of advice and this has to be at the very least the second book you've read that quotes these words. So, knowing this, I hope to not repeat the same things without showing you something new, not to show you the same things without saying something new and ideally be altogether original. For one, I will not talk about just one part of this famous set of sentences. Instead we will discuss all of them I will not combine them however instead we will break them down one by one until we have chewed every last bite of flavor from every word.

Just one second...

Love is patient. Sounds simple enough doesn't it. I'm very impatient. The funny thing is how my wife and I are impatient at opposite times and about different things. When I think of patience I think of waiting. I'm not a good waiter. I heard a great teaching once about waiting. The speaker taught about waiting on God. He talked about how waiting is not sitting at a red light with one foot on the brake and the other on the gas revving the engine so you can shoot the green light. It is not waiting for the food to cool down when you get it out of the oven pour a drink and take a bite knowing full well that it is still very hot. Usually what follows is that you've now burned your tongue in the process of your inability to wait, and be patient.

Love is patient, this means Love waits. Next time it's hard to be loving wait a moment. It's amazing how much difference one second makes.

My best friend and I used to play pool a lot when we were in high school and still try to do so every chance we get, that is whenever I go back for a visit. We used to be pretty good for the amount we played and we'd get pretty competitive. However, even some of your best competitors understand that it is important to be patient and to be tactical. Yet, we'd get in a rush and not make the right shot then get mad and therefore frustrated and from there it was all downhill. So we created the "one second or count to one rule" This was simple, take a breath before your next shot and say, one or better count one second, one, one thousand. Let's just say you'd be amazed at how many more shots we made when we did this and how much better we became and therefore more competitive yet we also learned the greatness of being patient, of waiting, if even only for just one second.

Serving selflessly

Love is kind. This probably seems oh so obvious. If you've experienced kindness you've experienced love. Has anyone ever done something for you just out of kindness? I have had the discussion with many friends if this is even possible! After all generally there are expectations and hopes tied to our acts of kindness. We hope to get something in return or at least recognized for our actions. We many times are kind only when it is easy, though it may be sincere, it is generally not something we do when it is difficult. I am a huge proponent that if we'd count to one and be a little more patient it'd be a lot easier for us to be kind. Let's talk first about what *not* to do.

The other day my wife hollers at me, "Honnnnnneeyyyy!" Now let me stop right there, usually I'd like to believe I am quick to respond and go see what she needs, or at the very least holler back, "Whaaat?" This at least gives her the opportunity to let me know if it's important. This night however, I was focused on packing for a trip I was taking for work the next morning (quite early the next morning may I add) and it was already getting later into the night. So, I replied to her, "Honnnneeey" with "I'm on the other side of the housssse!" Then I proceeded to mumble under my breath, she knows I'm on the other side of the house, why is she hollering at me from afar. You see, had I stopped and counted to one and repeated that thought I would have gone to her. After all, the key is 1. I usually go to her, 2. It didn't make sense that she was hollering at me from across the house when she knew I was focused on something important so that means 3. Ah, she was in need, it was something important.

I've come to realize when someone 'hollers' at us and we're not sure why this should be an immediate clue to the fact that they are in need. I mean, I believe my wife to be a self sufficient person. I believe her to be smart and to know me. I believe that she cares about me and understands if I'm doing something of which takes up my focus then I need time to focus on it. I believe also that to leave something of which we are focused on something of 'self' for the need of another is one of the most difficult things to do. It's like driving 100 mph down a straight two lane road and all of sudden during a short clearing in traffic both ways someone yells, "TURN AROUND!" It's enough to cause you to have an accident. Rather, we could easily, calmly, slow down, pull over and see what the need is and most likely turn around if the need justifies it.

Instead, I wasn't willing to turn around and didn't even slow down. Instead my response was more of an explanation of the obvious, "I'm going 100 miles per hour". I wonder if when I did this she was in the other room, on the other side of the house, thinking, "I know this, would I be yelling for you if it wasn't important?" Soon, I knew her need though she had to holler again and I did not serve selflessly until I had already gone frustratingly to learn that it had

been important. Next time, I hope that I will respond differently.
Next time I hope to take into account who she is, that she knows
me, and with my knowledge of her and that if she hollers, "Honey,"
I should go and see what I can do. The bag will still get packed,
we'll still get to our destination, even if we slow down and pull over.
When we get there we'll all be better off when we serve selflessly.

I know me too or I know me even more...

This thinking does definitely not Love. Look at two of the four
words in each phrase. They are I and me! In addition, when you
hear someone say 'I know' does it sound like they're connecting or
does it take away from the awesome revelation or emotion you just
had? When they say 'me too' which does it do? I've heard
psychiatrists report that in fact when people try to relate to you
often it is them giving themselves justification for something in
their life. So in your time of need, due to their envy, you end up
Loving them instead of them Loving you.

Let me state right now this is not something that is entirely wrong
in mind. I'm often glad when someone says they understand and
relate to me but often we just want to express ourselves. When you
accomplish something great, you want to hear congratulations, not,
wish I could do that. The first affirms and Loves. The second may
make you feel bad that you just did the 'great thing' you did. You
see it is my belief that we don't see these things as envy but as
meager attempts to encourage. When someone says, "I lost 20
pounds. I'm so excited and feel so much better." If you respond
with, "I always wanted to get into shape" it may be a way of saying,
"Wow that's great that you were able to lose 20 lbs and get so much
healthier, you look great. Many people struggle so much with that
and I'm sure it wasn't easy but you did it!"

Love does not envy – Because when we are envious we think of
ourselves not lovingly about the other person. We do this all the
time. "I always wanted a good job" "Good for you, I wish I could
go back to school, glad you were able to finish." Instead of, "You

104

did it! You finally got your dream job." Or, "You worked hard and got your degree."

I'm a huge proponent that the quickest way of reading our 'envy meter' is to check 'I' and 'me' at the door and begin to replace them with You and Your and work harder to end with a sincerely excited '!' and not a complacent frustrated '...'

Then what about that next line?

Love does not boast. Sharing an accomplishment doesn't have to be boasting. We share what we do and we ask others about them. It's conversation. Ideally in our asking about one another we give each other great opportunities to share about ourselves. You could say we show love by kindly, serving selflessly and patiently waiting for our opportunity to tell of our own story. Again, this works great when both persons are doing this so I hope the person you are thinking of is reading this too. In all seriousness I believe Love is like a smile. It's contagious. Let those who can do, let those who can't, begin to learn from those doing. Boasting is bragging. To me this is going on and on about what "I" did. To say I'm so excited I finally got a good job isn't I worked and worked and I climbed my way to the top! It isn't talking about what all you did to get what you wanted then going on and on about what you have.

In some cases yes, not mentioning it can be difficult. To state a fact and share an experience can be done in such a context that is respectful. If it is something that could hurt someone else then you might want to consider hers/his feelings and how they might be affected. If it is a close friend or family who knows how you've been working toward a goal, then sharing the achievement of that goal is not boastful. However, if on your first time meeting someone, you use accomplishments to build yourself up on a pedestal to look good for them rather than creating a place for mutual learning and conversation well that would be. I've recently been blessed with much good news, a five year anniversary with a wonderful woman, a new job, working on a book, and most recently news of a baby on the way!

I'm excited, however, if I knew someone struggling to have a child, I would consider for a moment if I should share my excitement, possibly at the least keeping it in check knowing that each time I mention it, it could be adding stress in her life in efforts toward having children. This could go for so many things. I've learned many times you can use your joy lovingly by 1.) Giving the glory to God and recognizing it as a gift, this helps you check the 'I' at the door. 2.) Try looking at how you can give others hope. For example, "I know you and your wife have wanted kids for so long. After five years Lisa and I are finally having children and we're in our 30's. You guys keep trying, after all that is the best part they say." Giving a grin and lightening the mood.

I recently read that stress of wanting kids is one of the biggest hindrances to having them! It's true about so many things. The more we want them, the harder it is. When others boast it can heighten our stress of wanting something similar and get in the way.

So I say Love does not boast but use experiences to relate in a way that lifts others up. Think on that next time something great happens. Ask how can I share this joy not just how can I tell everyone what I did?

One and the same

I'm going to cover this next one simply. Boasting is pride and pride is boasting. Being proud in some minds is very different than 'pride' as it is spoken here when we read, Love is not Proud. We could just as easily say, "Love is not arrogant, Love is not conceited, Love is not smug, or Love is not self-seeking or doesn't focus on self importance." You see I think we've pretty much covered that.

For those who are like myself, who always had a hard time with the whole "love is not proud" statement then let me ask, are these statements I have made co-existent with how you perceive being proud? In my case, I'm proud to say my wife and I have been married happily for five years. However, I am being arrogant if I say, well you should listen to what I've got to say, I've been happily married for five years, to someone who is struggling in their relationship. None of us have all the answers. In the same way we may be proud of someone else feeling joy from an accomplishment and this again is not prideful love. It's just that funny English language throwing a wrench at us when we read.

After all, when I looked up synonyms for proud, in addition to the ones just mentioned I found pompous, self-righteous, over confident, and big headed. However, when looking up prideful in a way that refers to having prideful love, like how I believe I am 'proud of my nephew' I found these words: glowing, complimentary, flattering, appreciative, and congratulatory.

Hope that helped clear up what is meant when we read in Corinthians 13:4 that Love is not proud.

Next verse, same as the first

Corinthians 5 says, "It is not rude, it is not self-seeking, it is not easily angered, it keeps no record of wrongs."

I think Love is not rude should be the clearest of all of these! Has anyone ever been rude to you? Of course they have. Did you feel loved? I'm not talking about tough love which can definitely seem rude. No, not that call you out when you need it sort of thing. I'm talking about random acts of rudeness. This is an act I think that is the easiest to get away with on a day to day basis in society. I say something rude about the lady to my left, the guy walks by me slamming me in the arm but doesn't slow down. Rudeness is commonly accepted and almost encouraged in our society. It's sometimes equalized and justified as being 'tough'. Well, you can be tough or you can love and still be strong. Because, I think you'll agree, Love is not rude.

Get this, it's not about you!

I know it's hard to believe but it's true. Don't turn away, get mad or throw your hands in the air. I'm only trying to remind us that Love is about others. "Love others as yourself." Sure we must Love ourselves and care for ourselves in such away that we can Love others. Still, the ultimate goal there is to be able to Love others. Even as the sentence preceding that one in Matthew 22:37 is Love God with all of your heart and mind and soul, the great commandment ends with loving others. After all, Christians look at Jesus as the embodiment of God's Love for the world. Did you catch that? The world! Not just the world that was here when Jesus was crucified, but the world that was here His whole life, before his life and following his life even 2000+ years later.

That's as "others" as I can imagine. For Jesus it was never about Him. It was always Love and Serve God then Love and Serve Others, all the others. He made it clear that everyone on the planet should be considered our neighbor when He said, Love thy neighbor. So maybe you're not a Bible person. No matter, let's go ahead and talk about you (and for that matter me and most all of us for a moment).

When you want someone to Love you, what is it you're asking for? A loving touch? A small token of appreciation? Some sincere time with someone who listens to you, who cares about you and what you share. Whatever it is you're looking for from that special someone, chances are it's for you, something that adds to your quality of life, lifts you up, and makes you feel good. Now then, let's reverse that. If you are to Love someone else, doesn't it reason to believe that you should consider what they're needs are? The need for a Loving touch. The need for a small token of appreciation. Some sincere time with someone who listens to them, who cares about them and what they have to share. Whatever it is they're looking for from that special someone, chances are it's for them, something that adds to their quality of life, lifts them up, and makes them feel good. In other words whenever, whomever we

Love it should be about them and not us. This is why many people appreciate eye contact so much. It shows you're attentive to them and not so easily distracted that it makes them and what they have to share seem unimportant. In addition, in today's world, it truly is very easy to become distracted and to be able to justify such action. So then, even more so, simply holding eye contact can be an action of Love.

Love is whenever we make it about others. The saddest thing is that many take love and aren't able to return it. So I say again, it is my hope and prayer that we would all begin to give Love as it is meant to be. If that was so, none of us would have a need because the need would be met. None of us would be looking for Love because it would be freely given. We could then concentrate on living life to the fullest as we were intended. I often say Jesus is the center of the Christian Faith. That faith teaches that God is Love and so you could say if we are to make God, whom is love, and His Son, Jesus, the embodiment of Love the center of our lives, then Love itself should be the center of all people and we should live outwardly, fully, completely. After all, Love is not self-seeking, it is others-seeking.

I love you he said as he stormed off, slammed the door and screeched the tires as he pulled away...

Anger and Love rarely mix. It is true one can have righteous anger. However, a prayer I often pray is, "Lord, let me be slow to anger and quick to Love." In the Lord's Prayer it reads, "Forgive us of our trespasses as we forgive those who trespass against us" My thought is for me, that means to forgive I must Love, to forgive, I should not hold on to anger, to not hold on to anger which isn't righteous, ideally, not being quick to anger however, instead discerning an understanding of why someone might have acted in a certain way or possibly just being willing to allow them the space to mess up and say something hurtful and to address it appropriately rather than with 'return fire' or remember that I have ran a red light too or whatever it might be.

I want to Love, first, in order to not be quick to anger which many times is led by strong and quick minded emotions and follows with a reaction that is that of which, I think we'd both agree, is probably not at all loving, but more of one that is rude. And, we already discussed the fact that Love is definitely not rude. So, an easy way to not be rude, it is to not quickly be angered. A final, note is often we say we love in the midst of being angry and rude. This is to mock the very word. If we are slow to anger maybe we can better express our pains and frustration in a more healthy way and also, maybe we'd have lower blood pressure, less busted door hinges and longer lasting tires. Love is not easily angered.

It's not MY fault, it's YOUR fault!

It's often hard for me to talk about my past relationships. After all, I now can truly see all the times I made mistakes in them. I can look back in hindsight and know the hurt that I caused and see the ways that I did not Love. In addition to these things I now can see many more, of my wrongs as opposed to the few that I saw back then. In doing that, I can find patterns and areas of concern to be aware of in current relationships and especially in my marriage. One of those is the danger of blame, throwing fault and claiming to be right regardless of discerning what is really of importance and the cause/root of the feelings in that moment. Not long ago I caught myself thinking things along the lines of, "I do this and this and that, and I don't know why I should also have to do _____. (Fill in the blank)

Immediately I flashed back to past relationships. Mine and others I had seen do this. Claiming all the stuff I did as if the other person does nothing or not nearly as much as I. Now remember that this is about three years into my marriage that I caught myself doing this. Immediately I began to think on all the things my wife does. She encourages me in my endeavors. She works full time as do I. She cooks for us daily. We tend to share many responsibilities, though she tends to do a little more of the general house cleaning and daily things like dishes and making the bed. However, at this moment I felt she had called on me to do more of the daily tasks or they weren't being done and I had to do them. My head thought, I already help in these areas and I do all the yard work (we lived in Virginia then, so we had a good size yard). I take care of the bills and the cars. Are you getting the idea? The fact is she was not really doing 'nothing'. She was doing a little less than she usually did.

There were a couple of things happening here. One, she was a little depressed. This resulted in less motivation. Poor pitiful me wanted to throw blame and claim some glory (that's the bad kind of pride) rather than provide Love by serving with a Loving heart. Also, she didn't want me to do it all. I have since learned, thanks to Gary Chapman's book, The Five Love Languages, that my wife's Love language is 'quality time' followed closely by 'acts of service'. I knew this before but I've learned more about the dialects of these languages. She loved when I took three minutes to make the bed. She appreciated that if she cooked, I helped with dishes. Or, if I got the mail I put it away and tossed the junk and I don't mean toss it on the dinner table over a few days time. These small acts of service showed my wife Love.

The first emotion I responded with was due to my being easily angered from there I began to hold fault and Love does not keep a list of wrongs. This means I also, don't bring this or other things from the past up as a way to get what I want or to use as return ammunition in a confrontation. This simply says, 'Once you've hurt me, I'm never letting it go. I'm going to keep it in my pocket and pull it out whenever I'm easily angered and feeling prideful even if it's just rude to do so. Are you seeing the domino affect of these and why they're all pulled together in one place to let us know how to Love by letting us know how not to love? Sounds like, we have our own laundry list or record of wrongs. Something to remember…

Evil is good?

Go ahead, say it. Don't ask it, say it. Evil is good. Did you just raise an eyebrow? Are you wondering what point is about to be made? Maybe you're like, "Oh boy what is this about?" Or maybe you're one of a few thinking I know some evil that I could do that's real good. Or maybe you're one of the even more few who remembers something you once did that was evil and you thought it was good until the results came from those actions. I'm going to speak on life experience once again.

I know many men and women who struggle with abstaining from sex in a relationship where they are attracted to each other. This can be a working relationship, friendship, or a potential life mate. It doesn't matter. What matters is that once we feel close to someone, we assume anything we do in connection with that relationship can't be bad. If she tells him, "I really love that you listen attentively." it must be a compliment, right? What about, when he says, "You look great, have you lost weight, what a cute dress, new haircut, etc…?" It must be simple flattery right? Or can both of these possibly not be good and encouraging but instead flirtatious? Are they lingering towards an inappropriate relationship based on wrong motivation and emotion?

If and I emphasize *if* it is in fact, a simple uplifting comment with sincere, and I also place emphasis on sincere, motivation then that is fine. If not, let's call it what it is, evil. Evil is the anti-good. Funny though, it can look good, feel good and that can cause some real confusion.

I love a good slice of pizza, a chili cheeseburger and fries, and many other foods that any dietician would tell you are NOT GOOD for me. So why do I say, MMMM this is so GOOD when I have it? It's appealing and fills a moment with very short term joy. I'm 40 pounds heavier than only a few short years ago when I was in the best shape of my life. Sadly that includes having lost 10-15 lbs over the last year or so. So what really is the definition of good? I gained most of that weight on the road. It was just easier to eat all that 'good' food that was at the truck stops along the highway or the fast food places we ran through as we tried to make the best time possible. Vending machines were comforting as well when I was tired after a long day and crashed at the hotel for the night.

While many things in life are good for a moment, not choosing those things can be good for the long run, maybe even a lifetime. I'm sure you have perfect vision when looking back at a choice you made to please a desire in the moment rather than that which was truly good for you.

And so beware, Love does not delight in evil but rejoices with the truth.

So when you choose to love anyone, including yourself, ask yourself, what truth do I find in doing this.

What Love is found in this?

In the gospels we read where Jesus responds to a man who has just called him 'Good Teacher'. Jesus said to him, "Why do you call Me good? No one is good except God alone." Mark 10:18

A common love of all creatures

It is not uncommon to see the wildlife on the Discovery channel fighting with both their own kind, predators and so forth in defense of another. It can be for their mate, their children or simply another animal running in their pack. Still, you will see them protecting. When I think of someone showing me love by protecting me, I think of my parents and my sister. I think of how they cared more about protecting me than how I felt, even about them. This protectiveness is an interesting way to show love. Who do you defend? If someone you Love was being verbally attacked, would you defend them? Would you step in and protect them? How do you protect someone you Love before they are attacked or placed in a compromised position? Many times I believe good education is good protection. If we can be taught well and how to implement that which we are taught we can protect ourselves from many hurts in life. Love always protects. It is my hope these words you read will protect you and others from the pain of not being able to Love in fullness and in truth. I am thankful for the Love of my parents, sister, wife and those friends who have all been willing at different times to step in and protect me from evil in one form or another.

How can I be sure?

You don't have to be. Just trust. Love always trusts. When trust is broken we find it very hard to Love. It is easy to blame, easy to anger but very difficult to Love. Love however always trusts. At this juncture in my writing I'm in my family's home town and my wife remains at our home some 1500 miles away. My father is in the hospital and I am here in support. It has been just over a week of a roller coaster ride and my wife and I have barely been able to have phone time together. Also, I'd like to mention that she is expecting our first child. She is emotional and has mentioned nightmares almost daily. It's hard to be away from the one you Love. For us, I know it is especially difficult. We really enjoy as much time together as possible.

For the first many years of our marriage we worked together so when we moved near New York City and began working different hours in different jobs in different towns, it definitely was an adjustment. In all of these situations a new line of trust had to be relied upon. We worked away from each other and brought home stories of both men and women we worked with. How would we be influenced by these men and women? Most certainly somewhere along the way some guy would be flirtatious with her and some woman with me and how would we respond. Let's also remember that we spend on average sleeping eight hours a day and spend eight or more hours at work leaving us with about six hours with our spouse if we're lucky after commuting, variations in work schedules and so on. This means we can easily end up being around our co-workers more than our wives and husbands. We must Love our spouse and therefore we must trust our spouse. In being away from each other in emotional times where we are used to being support for one another it is very difficult. We are both looking for someone to lean on.

My sister and I are leaning on one another a great deal. In many relationships however, a person has no sibling to rely on for that support. They turn to a 'friend'. That friendship changes to more, if even for but a short time. We've all heard of the stories of broken relationships due to such things. This is why it can be so hard to trust. We just read however, Love always trusts. Trust is a lot like faith. It's there for that which is unseen. I have trust in and hold trust in my wife even from 1500 miles away. Lack of trust creates opportunities for destruction as well. This goes not only for your relationship but the effect it can have on others.

I have known people who have actually spied on their spouse or person of interest for very weak reasons. They had a hard time trusting. You might say they had a hard time loving. I knew of one person who invited a friend along for her stake out. Her friend however, was in a good relationship, having been married for just over a year. The two women began hanging out. Many of their friends began going into rants about men. Eventually the influence began to impact the married woman who was already having other personal struggles. I believe it helped open the door for a divorce that came later. It's very hard to trust when you let 'question' enter your heart. Love always trusts.

If Love is to always trust it must act right too. In my past I have been in relationships when another woman would come along and be a definite distraction. Via friendship and/or a physical attraction I'd begin to think inappropriately about this person. I have since realized much better how to handle such dangers and that is a teaching for another day. When these things happen, we tend to let our fantasies run wild even if we keep our actions in check. This opens a door for our mind to wander. The next time our significant other talks about someone from work of the opposite sex, we begin to wonder, what if she likes him. She sounds like she likes him. The way he talks about her gets him so excited, she must excite him. Sometimes these thoughts can be warranted. Confronting the person about them for reasons of accountability and checks and balances is good while, questions due to a lack of trust are another thing all together. Love always trusts.

Don't give up hope...

As I mentioned, right now I'm with my dad in the ICU and my family has had many discussions about his health and his future. We all Love him very much. We're not giving up on any part of his recovery. We understand what can and can't happen. We're not fantasizing by being hopeful. I'm not sure why it's important for some to believe something will or won't 100% happen. Maybe they just want to be able to have 'a definite.' Maybe it's to make things easier to deal with. Whatever the reason, we can believe for the best and be prepared for the worst.

I'm going to go on a lighter note to explain this. I'm going to use a sports metaphor in hopes that the general demographic studies of persons likely to read this book allow for it. I am a huge Dallas Cowboys fan and have been since the age of five. So I was there for the good, the bad, the ugly and the Super Bowl wins along the way. No matter what happens each season I'm there rooting them on. We have definitely seen some ugly seasons including 1989, a 1-15 year. OUCH. I will say though, that one win, was sweet. We were up against the Washington Redskins and I'm sure they were hopeful of a win against a team that was being beaten by most everyone that year. May it be noted two years later the team set a then team record thirteen wins and the following year after that they won the Super Bowl decisively.

The reason I bring this up is that each game I was hopeful. Maybe it was for a win; maybe it was for what was ahead or to see my favorite player have success. You see my point is we can always have hope even when the odds are against us. It's my opinion that hope is important for the long term. In the short term it seems the odds are greater stacked against us however, over enough time we have more and more opportunities for success. I'm sure each game in 1989 was difficult. But in the long run the Cowboys were in for an incredible span of ten years of winning seasons and three Super Bowl victories. What if everyone involved lost hope because of a bad game, fifteen bad games to be exact?

Love always hopes. When we get into a fight with someone we Love, when someone we Love hurts, when we hurt, when the odds are stacked against us, if we can get through that moment, that experience in life and stay with it for the long term, things have a better chance of turning around. Love always hopes.

What really always perseveres?

I'm not sure I know of anything that really perseveres through everything. Sure I've seen cars run hundreds of thousands of miles and yet parts must be replaced and eventually they all go to a junk yard or get recycled. Great men have come and gone. Great companies have fallen to other great companies as have great countries! Super glue, nails, steel, all I have seen falter at some point. Love on the other hand always perseveres. Go ahead and scoff at the idea of Love always persevering. Are you done?

Ok, let's talk about this. Does it Love to anger? No. Does it Love to hold onto a list of wrongs? No. I won't go through them all, however, if you're thinking of the person who said they loved you and they were abusive or maybe parents who said they loved each other and hurt each other and ended up in divorce or whatever is the case then lets remember what Love is.

Love is a choice.

In relationships with those of whom we care deeply when we mess up and stop loving them and do something self seeking for our own desire that is not in line with Love anyway. When we do this people say but, "He loved her, how could he have an affair?" That's simple, in all actuality, he didn't Love her. Not then at least, not at that time. Maybe he loved her before and afterward hoped for another shot at loving her. The other thing I'd like to mention is that when Love is real and sincere I have seen even the worse verbal abuse change into words of honesty and caring. She stops telling him he can't and starts telling him he can. I have seen affairs not forgotten but definitely forgiven and the list of wrongs cleared. Scripture says, Faith without works is dead. I believe Love is much the same way. When our works are in line with our Love we can have faith that Love always perseveres.

Repeat (Love never fails)

If you're wondering what I want to say about "Love never failing" then by all means, read that last section again then roll right into... the question of, "Always?"

Always!?!?

When I read this section of scripture I can't help but ask, "Always?" Really? I mean Love *always* this and *always* that? Seriously, always? I mean I can't always and she doesn't always. He doesn't always, they sure didn't always. I know so and so from church doesn't always and mom and dad didn't always and my sister is great but did she always? What about those relationships of my past, they certainly didn't always or they would not be relationships of the past! Then as I say this I realize. I'm not talk about love in those questions. I'm talking about people. People may not *always* be able to do anything, but Love can. To me this has a three fold point.

Love as an entity and an action that we take and do is always able to result in the ways mentioned. However, we must first know the definition, second accept it and apply it and finally allow it to manifest in our relationships and trust in it.

The next part of my understanding from when I began to search this realization is that we tend to blame love for that which is a fault of people. And since we are already beginning to see we lack a strong knowledge of what love is and how to love we actually are blaming people for not doing something they don't know how to do! You have probably felt the brunt of this yourself. You've been told, "If you loved me you'd do _____. (Fill in the blank) You stood there dumbfound, wondering, "What? I do love you, I just (say it with me) *didn't know.*"

I could throw out a bunch of metaphors about using the right person or wrong person for the right or wrong job. However, I don't think there is a need for that. It is probably pretty evident to both you and I, that it's difficult to get mad at somebody for doing the wrong thing when they didn't know better in the first place. So why do we place the blame on people when they can't love? Funny enough, for the same reason, we don't know better. Well, I didn't know better but I believe I do know better now. And as a good friend of mine says she was taught, "When you know better, do better." The final piece to this is that we can say Love always because this is scriptural. And, it is discussed that God is Love. So, where we see Love in this scripture we can inter exchange God.

God is patient, God is kind. He does not envy, He does not boast, He is not proud. He is not rude, He is not self-seeking, He is not easily angered, He keeps no record of wrongs. God does not delight in evil but rejoices with the truth. He always protects, always trusts, always hopes, and always perseveres. He never fails.

Let me note we can talk theology another time. I think some will want to combat me about God not keeping a record of wrongs. You see He has records but He also provided a way for them to be forgiven and wiped clean. This is why I feel we can place God in that line as well as others.

After reading this I think we might find to seek out how to love we must seek love itself. In order to do so we must seek God himself. Matthew 6:33 states, "But seek ye first the kingdom of God, and His righteousness; and all these things shall be added unto you." I love this scripture because I think it is a great 'center point'. We all need a center to start from. Start from the outside and work your way in and may times we wear out to quickly. Start from the inside out and one thing seems to propel us to the next. If we can seek out Love itself and let Love penetrate our hearts, our minds and our souls until it has changed the very way we live our lives then we can be filled with Love. Our Love will be seen in us. We read in John 13:35: "By this shall all men know that you are my disciples, if you have love one for another".

You often hear that we should be known by our love. So if Love is an action, an effort made then we should be known by such. And this means we will be known by the evidence of the Love, of the actions in our lives now transformed by the understanding we have. An understanding of Love and our willingness to choose to implement that knowledge and turn it into action in our lives. We may not always be able to do this, but we understand that when we do, Love is not inconsistent, Love continues to never fail even though we may at times fail to Love.

Love VS. Compassion

My wife and I attend a weekly study group. One week our group dove into the subject of compassion. It was an excellent discussion with all parties going deeper into the idea of being more compassionate in our world. One person commented that "compassion is what we do for strangers while love is what we do for family." What do you think our friend meant by this comment? My first thought is this: Our friend was implying in that moment that, Love is required of those of whom we are related. We don't choose to Love our family, our parents, siblings, spouse or children. We do however have to choose to Love the stranger in need on the side of the road, on the sidewalk hurting or any time we go out of our way to help someone we don't know who is in need.

I was a little set back by this thought process. It implies that we don't have a choice in helping those we know. It implies that it is somehow inherent and even automatic. I'm sure most, if not everyone who is reading this can attest to, someone in our family who has hurt someone else of our blood or in relation to them and us. While for some of us it may certainly be easy to Love our family because of our relationship, it is still a choice, as we've been discussing to get up and move into action in a way that results positively for them regardless of what we do or don't get from it. For many I've actually found it's easier for them to Love others that they are not related to. It's as if they have an internal pull towards strangers and helping others and yet sometimes do not see the obvious ways they can and need to care for the persons in their very home.

On the other hand, we might want to consider what this might also say about how a person generally thinks about compassion vs. love initially. Can we not have compassion for our family? I believe that compassion moves us to Love. Or at least it should, shouldn't it? When we opened up about different areas of our heart and thoughts we found it difficult to be compassionate, I brought up my knee jerk reactions to people in a variety of cases. Such are those all too quick responses to my wife, my sister and the stranger in that car who just about ran out in front of me. When she does not recognize how important something is to me and doesn't put it first, my first thought is not how can I show her Love. I do not move from compassion to think first why is it she is not responding in a way she clearly must see I need. For if I was to be moved with compassion, I might move next with Love. I might would say, "That's ok honey." or I might would ask, "Baby, don't you see how important this is, and how much I want you to share it with me. Usually you would want to share these moments, are you ok?" Instead however, I move with anger which translates into a very unloving attitude along with unloving words, which may be simply "FINE!" and my walking away. In the moment of my wants, desires and my interest I have a very difficult time being compassionate and therefore my ability to love is blocked by this wall I have allowed to come between me and the other person.

This is the case also if it is a stranger. I have seen persons do some crazy things on the road. Being a New York City 'B & T', I have also seen some pretty crazy things happen on the sidewalks.

However, I ask you and me, as we sit here and think of all the crazy things we've even seen people do just this very day to entertain the question, "Have I ever even once done one dumb thing?" Have I ever cut someone off? Have I ever stopped walking in a crowd? Have I ever not been paying attention while messing with the radio or talking on the cell phone? Sure, I'd be willing to bet we all have done something that got in the way of someone else. I don't know about you but I can think of many times I have thought, "Sorry, I didn't mean to do that." or "Oh man, I was the dumb one there!"

If I could have, I would have told the person, "I'm sorry about that, I clearly was not paying attention and hurt you, got in your way, etc..." For those of you that have ever caused any pain or had a car wreck in which the accident was in any small or great way your responsibility, you can agree, having that person show you some compassion would be great. And that compassion when shown would be an amazing way to Love.

However, as much as I have cried out, prayed, begged and hoped for compassion in those moments when I hit someone or almost hit someone while driving or stopped walking here or there in a crowd or whatever the case, I do not equally provide that compassion to others. Maybe if we showed more compassion to all persons, both related and not, we would then see the effect of the Love that follows and that compassion represents so often.

Compassion and Forgiveness

As we discussed compassion in our group we moved on to forgiveness. I think forgiveness is an amazing way to not only show others Love but to also Love ourselves. In the Lord's Prayer it says "Forgive us of our sins as we forgive those who have sinned against us." What if we used the word love there instead? Lord, Love us as we love others… What if we are compassionate and therefore are able to forgive and from that, Love is shown by our actions. In response we Love others, we Love ourselves and we can say in the same way, Lord, Love us. What are we asking for? We are asking for forgiveness, mercy, and grace. What is He asking us to do for others by loving them? Freely give them forgiveness, mercy and grace.

CHAPTER 17

You can't take it with you...or can you?

Often you will hear the phrase "you can't take it with you." This came to mind recently and I began asking both Christian and non-Christian friends if they agreed with this statement. The resounding answer was yes of course. I mean if there is an afterworld you probably will not wake up and still have access to your bank account. Even if you're buried with your car, as some people are, you likely won't wake up on the other side driving it. So the question I began to pose, to those who do believe in an afterlife, is there anything you can take with you? Is there anything you can do to impact others to have on the other side?

I'm going to ask you to ponder on that thought for just a moment. Maybe even consider pondering on it for a while.

For those who are video game lovers (and for that matter even if you're not) there is one thing that is more important than anything. Look at video games like Pac-Man, Galaga, Space Invaders, Legend of Zelda, pinball or racing games and many others that provide you with extra time. The fact is no matter what weapon you can claim, no matter what you grab a hold of that will get you points, the most important thing to hold on to or to gain more of is...? Life. Life gives you another chance. Life determines when the game is not over. Can you imagine a game where you could get eternal life? Where if you gained it the game never ends? You could continue to play as long as you like. Life is the most important weapon you might say you could have. So if it is the most important weapon you can gain, maybe it is also the strongest weapon you can give others. Do you have the answer to what can be taken with us?

Life, Life is the one thing that we take on. If in fact, as I believe there is a life beyond this world, then what kind of life if any will you have on the other side? What kind of life are you helping others to have here where we are? What greater love is there than to give life? Loosely translated Romans 5:7 says that rarely will someone give their life even for a righteous man, or in John 15:13

we read, the greatest thing any man can do is give his life for another.

So I challenge you to look at how you love others and even yourself. Are your actions those, that you call loving, giving life? Do they help give life, a life which is full and uplifting?

Love aids eternal life not eternal death. Do your actions give life as God intended or does it take it in exchange?

This is love, to give life in the actions we choose to make each moment of each day.

Notes:

Memories + Renewed understanding = Greater Love

Love keeps those you've lost close to your heart. I see a young person growing, I see an old man singing as he sits with a lady in his life. I see a young couple pulling each other closely. Love makes me see myself and others in that young person. It brings back memories of doing this or that alone or with those others. Love makes these memories so clear, I relive them, and I relive the love of those days and those whose lives are intertwined with mine. I relive the life gone by and make it part of today and I love those memories and those people in my life all over. I stop and embrace them in the moment in my heart all over and pray for them. The young couple reminds me of those loves (in the wrong sense of the word in my many earlier given definitions) gone by. Yet still, there is a beautiful memory of each from a life I have lived. A life filled with pain and joy and growth from all that fell in between. The older couple makes me think of my parents and those in their life and many others as well. And with each passing moment the memories fill my heart and cause me to smile. The funny thing is as I sit here, in this little coffee shop, those around me don't even know the memories they are bringing to my mind and that they are the reason for the light in my eye. So, soak up the Love being provided to you like solar rays provide energy every day all around you.

Can you love an inanimate object then?

You may be surprised to hear my answer is yes. While the focus of this book is to better define the meaning if love specifically in terms of relationships it is also to help us think in more depth about the very definition of love itself. We have established that love is a verb. We have established that love is not something we feel but something we do. I believe this is why when Paul said in 1 Corinthians things like "if I have this or that but do not have love, or if I can do this or that but do not have love.

Often scriptures such as these and ones like the repetition found in James 2: 17, 20 and 26 state faith without works is dead are scrutinized. However, few argue that the matters of the faith, Christianity teaches is one of the heart. On that note what if the works spoken about were not done out of duty because we are simply working to please God and do good things? What if instead the works spoken of are works of Love. Works done from the heart to one another is because it is showing an action of love. Imagine giving of ourselves so that others will not be left in need.

Faith hope and love... Or the greatest of these...

You may have heard this about faith, hope and love. These are all ways that you can give however the greatest of them is Love. This reminds me of something I remember learning in school. Just because a tiger a lion and a panther are all cats, not all cats belong in one of these groups. Interestingly enough having hope without recognizing the Love of someone seems impossible. Receiving or giving grace requires the act of Love. However, you may ask whenever we love is the act of grace or giving hope considered or even involved. Let's run with that thought. Whenever you felt Love did it give you hope? Maybe you didn't consciously think about it then. Do so now. What about grace. When you have received acts of Love did the person performing those act show you grace?

CHAPTER 18

What is truth?

I have to say to truly help us redefine "Love" we must also be sure we have the correct understanding of other words. One of those is Truth.

In John 8 you will read that upon certain circumstances what follows is this, "you will know the truth, and the truth will set you free." I'm sold that a lot of us don't like the truth. A popular phrase is, "The truth hurts." How about, "You can't handle the truth!" You see, the truth usually means change, acceptance and other things we don't like. Truth rarely says, yep, you're all good, doing things the best way, keep on keeping on. Nope, generally Truth says, that is a lie, you're lying to yourself and others or you're being lied to. We don't like lies, or at least I don't. I don't like to be called a liar, to call others liars or to think I've been lied to and what's worse didn't even know it! I often think of the movie the Matrix when I think of Truth. Did Truth trap or free Neo?

Depending on how you look at this it may well determine how you really feel about accepting and viewing truth in reality. At a young age I found out a product I had always been told to enjoy and consume a great deal of was actually hurting me more than helping me. My mother and I were extremely surprised when the Doctor gave us this information. We weren't entirely lied to, as this product does tend to help many persons. Still, this was causing me to hold on to extra weight and gain weight more quickly than if I consumed less or possibly none of this product. The tough part is that it's part of almost every meal in some way or at the least 1 meal a day. It was amazing, I began curbing my intake and it made an incredible difference. I've learned a lot about how various products affect my body. What we speak of today is about our mind and our spirit. It is about how some things affect every facet of who we are. If we are told, the truth is, when you feel attracted to someone, when you begin to feel a connection to someone based on some common ground and fun interaction and that is called being in love,

131

then we begin to base Love itself on these feelings then this and this alone is what we think is the Truth.

What's amazing is most people including myself have been caused more pain than joy, more damage than good from this line of understanding. Much like the product I was consuming, it could be that many of us have gotten lied to. However, just like it has been hard over the years for me to curb my intake of this common and beloved product, we might have to make some very hard changes in order to have a much healthier Love in our relationships of all kinds.

What is good for you? What is bad for you? What do you believe is true?

If we are not willing to learn the real truth then we will continue to act on lies. We will continue to do what we want right now rather than possibly not do right now what we should to get what we want for later. We can eat whatever we crave, but if it's always pizza and ice cream and beer we can assume it is likely that we will not become healthier. So if we want to be healthier and feel better through physical health we can not continue to simply sleep in instead of working out and eat the aforementioned food and drink and expect any different. I can use analogy after analogy but I will not. I will refer to one of my favorite expressions I have heard again and again and think explains our actions in denying Truth the best; "The definition of insanity is doing the same thing again and again and expecting a different result." As long as we commit the same actions in the same situations with similar/same environments we can not expect something different to occur. However, if we accept that we must learn to change how we think, to renew our minds, we can change lies to Truth and we can Love and be Loved like we always hoped for. No, better, we can Love and be Loved in ways that we never knew were possible.

No such thing as 'in love'? Ok, not exactly.

I'm not saying there's no such thing as being in love. Ok, so I have said that, but allow me to clarify what I mean by using the word 'no'. In that sentence it is as dangerous as using words like none and never to loosely. What I need to clarify is that the feelings you get that trigger us to feel the in love euphoria is not what we should base our relationship decisions on. In many cases in life we are or we do have to look beyond some happy tingly good feelings and do things for other reasons. I've caught myself mad at the world or at least someone in the world and suddenly I don't give up my seat on the subway, hold the door open as I pass through or other similar acts of simple everyday kindness. Instead I go off of my feelings.

You may remember earlier I spoke of my time at the hospital with my dad and not losing hope. My dad went on to pass away and I learned you can feel angry and still have peace and joy. It was amazing. You see inside I was hurting and angry for many reasons at many people including myself and a little with God. But I was also getting to spend time with family and friends as well as some alone time for soul searching. To not set the hurt and anger aside and act on joy and real Love for others and even real Love for myself and not selfishness would have only added to my loss. Real Love is a decision while in love is a sudden rarely controllable emotion. As I got off the train I thought to myself, I'm in love with my wife! I had a moment of that euphoria but it is her showing me her ongoing true Love and acts of said Love and our sharing in real decision based on thought out, cared for Love that triggered this. So when it comes to being in love vs. having Love and giving and receiving Love I am only saying each one has a place in our lives. We should be careful to discern upon which one we are making life changing decisions, which are many of our daily decisions in the relationships of all kinds around us.

CHAPTER 19

Learning from renewed definitions

I have learned that Love as it should be is both much stronger and much more fragile all at the same time. Emotional "in love" tugs at a part of us that we do not understand and rarely if ever have any control over. Instead, it just pulls at the nerve center of our emotions making us hurt, laugh, cry, give all we can then give up on everything. I recently compared it to sleep in a talk with a friend. I have always been frustrated with sleep. I said, "It gets in the way of so many things I want and could do." However, my friend responded, it's kind of nice. I said it's like love, but what I should have said is that it's like the emotions of being in love. You see sleep is necessary. In love is not necessary but seems to happen to us none the less. Love many will argue is an absolute necessity. Regardless if this is the case it certainly is different than the reflex reaction of feelings we have in a generic connection with others. Real Love is actually our daily choosing. So can we just easily be thwarted in our choices?

When something is automatic, a reflex it can not be stopped. If there is an automated reaction to an action then what is special about that? If you have a nearly automated overwhelming response of attraction to someone then what is special about that? They speak or something you see makes you think of them and *uncontrollably* you get weak in the knees. I'm not saying it's not nice and doesn't feel good, but what makes it stand apart. I have had these feelings for a lot of people in my life. All of those people were special in one way or another to me and in my life. However, the feelings themselves were not entirely unique? If you think about it, what makes a relationship unique is what the people in the relationship do with their emotions, their attitudes and so forth. It is when two people make a daily conscious choice to Love in their actions, their words, and their attitude with a simple smile or kiss even when rushed. They stop and look at the other and make sure they know they are loved. Think about what set aside the most special of relationships. Was it feelings that were not controllable?

Did you do something without thought? Were your responses prompted from absolute euphoria?

I'm sure anyone reading this has experienced relationships of some sort. You know how early on you do things because of the automated response of excitement, attraction, and adventure of the unknown. You enjoy and soak up that you have found something new, a connection to someone who looks at you starry eyed and you look at them the same in return. You do not choose to touch them, your immense sexual attraction would not allow for anything less! You do not choose to buy them something, whenever you see almost anything you relate it to them and can not imagine otherwise! You do not choose to spend time with anyone else, because you can not imagine a moment without them! Notice all these reactions are the automated responses you have based on feelings you can not avoid. However, what if in a hurry, with other things on your mind, you cleared your head and gently touched the other person out of affection. How much more wonderful is that touch then the one coming from your mind and heart chasing after the result of a physical craving?! What if for a moment you stopped to clear your mind and really listen to the person(s) in your life so that when they mentioned that one thing that means so much to them, you would connect it and do it or buy it for them when the opportunity comes? How much more wonderful is that gift or action than the one done just because you basically want to buy them everything! I have to say I'm going through this a bit right now with my newly born daughter. I could just buy her everything, but instead I'm holding back and trying to get only what she needs or that will be special for years to come. I want to wait so I can watch, listen and learn what it is she will see as special and as loving. It is much more special to choose than to simply react like a program that is automated.

CHAPTER 20
Yet how delicate are our choices, how fragile are they...

My realization however is that as beautiful and as amazing and potentially strong is this real Love of choices made not responses automated it is also quite fragile. Since it is not automated we can as quickly choose in any given moment not to do what is needed as well. This does not love someone. So in each opportunity we choose not to love someone we begin to undo the bond, the love and the unity of the relationship. We must be cautious, to choose wisely. We must always be aware of our choices and the results of our actions. Much like our diet we can get away with making a bad choice now and then but it won't take long before too many will take a toll and can even mean the death of us. I believe that where the scriptures say that Jesus came so that we could live life and live it to the fullest, we should couple that with the words, you shall know the truth and the truth shall set you free. If we live a life of truth as it should be and not necessarily with simply the information we've been given or by the reflexes of our emotions we can truly live and live to the fullest a life nearly unimaginable by most.

We curse and we praise with the same lips

There is a Bible scripture that has stuck with me for some time now. It is referring to how we will praise the Lord and then curse in the very next breath. This is appalling to me, to think in two instances separated only by a breath that as humans we lose control of our tongue. For that matter isn't it much more appalling when one moment we do something loving and turn right around and do something that contradicts that action. This shows us that it is more than just a problem of our words.

In James 3 we read that a man who can tame his tongue can tame all parts of his body. Being that I've been called a talker I have always thought a lot about this statement in scripture. It has helped me re-shape how I speak and in doing so, has also reshaped how I listen. When I can tame my tongue I see positive change.

Until today I had difficulty in understanding how this pertained to those "quiet people." Then I realized maybe they should be cautious or concerned with the lack of production they are getting from this small but powerful muscle. Could it be that in order to tame our tongues it is like taming a horse? It is both important for it to respond to go this way or that as it is to stop. Could it be this was a way to show us how important two way communication is? To begin to understand that it is about more than just our tongue. That is simply where it begins. It continues in the results of the actions.

CHAPTER 21
Faith and Works

Earlier we discussed how in Biblical scripture Paul writes, works without faith is fruitless. It is also clear that works alone will not get us closer to God. Let's replace God and Faith with Love in that sentence. Let's also change the word works with action a word better used to understand the point in my humble opinion. "Love without action is dead. However, action alone will not get us closer to Love. We must love in action and not move (take action) as part of our love as well. You might think well *I DO* all kinds of things but she still doesn't see that I love her. You might say *He Does* lots of *good things* but I don't feel love. When we simply do what is easy for us to do and do not recognize the needs of others it is questionable how much we love.

We give lip service and say we love but do not follow through with our actions to listen and meet the others needs then it will be hard for them to believe our love is real. We must be willing to leave our comfort zone when necessary; we must be willing to do more than just the things that are easy for us. It is important we see what that person considers love. It is equally important we look at one another and see where they are coming from, what they are capable of and work with each other, exactly where we are at.

Note - Love is the works of faith:

These works will be different in different times for each of us. Though we have faith or trust in our best friend and our actions should prove this faith and trust that that may look different for me than you. The same would apply for family members and our religious faith as well. Someone recently pointed out that acceptance in regards to this thought process is very important. Often we're told, it's ok to give what you're capable of giving but yet we still walk away feeling guilty about what we can not give. It is so important that we Love in truth, sincerity and confidence. Not in judgment, abrasion, and self righteousness. It is the latter that both encourages and sometimes incriminates those feelings of guilt. Instead let us Love one another and in that Love let there be faith and trust and actions that prove that faith and trust. When we break that trust or do not see it, may we speak words of encouragement and truth yet hold steady in our confidence and understanding. We do not have to be perfect nor do we have to be pompous to be ok with who we are.

Our comfort in our own selves comes from loving ourselves. And in that, we will be able to Love others better and encourage their ability to better care for themselves. In turn they will then be able to Love others better. For years the effect of the lie of love has snowballed in a very wrong direction. Now we all are facing the repercussions of that and will continue to do so as long as the false is considered the truth if we do not turn minds around to renew and think different, to re-define Love.

For those who believe in the Christian faith we must remember that most wrong doing by those who are working to walk a life like Jesus walked is not done with well thought out intention but is instead done with quick reflex reaction based on their life and how they have become or based on us an how we've become. This is a result of sin in our world. Without going into a lot of theology and making this all about faith we must recognize that if we believe in sin as spoken about in the Bible then we understand it has an effect on us all. And even if you do not, you most surely recognize we all have 'our issue'. Yours and mine may be completely different. This is why we get, "Well, I do not understand why he can't just do the dishes when he dirty's them, I do it every time and then I end up doing his dishes!" While he says, "Why can't she just fill up the gas tank when it starts to get low? Every time I get in the car, it's low and I have to fill it up!" Now, those are very simple examples of thousands of things that we all do differently. Ways we think about things differently. And how we take different actions in different situations. Instead, we should go, you know maybe her dad always filled the gas tank for her and she just doesn't think about it. Maybe

144

every time he did the dishes he was told he didn't do a good enough job and now he thinks why do them, or because I mentioned how a little something didn't come off that plate that one time he feels judgment all over again.

Hmm, what if we had compassion, communicated and learned about one another? What would it look like if we focused on each others strengths and encouraged each other in our weaknesses? How about getting to know each other beyond the action and getting to know the cause. How about listening more and speaking less. Stopping assumptions and learning the truth. Doesn't that sound more loving than what we tend to see, and even do our selves on a daily basis? That is just a step in redefining Love.

Notes:

CHAPTER 22

Communication is key

I'm betting you are not a talker. You may be and if so, this might be a bit easier for you. If you are not a person whose love language is words then it is likely even more so that you are not a talker. It is very likely in my observation of this world that more often than not people do not like to actually talk. It is why churches across America have begun having life groups, small groups, cell groups. Call them what you want. My wife and I attend them. They're great for many reasons. For one they are just good therapy sessions. You bring people together, give them a common ground. It could be a book to discuss a certain subject or whatever. Then you provide them with some basic ground rules for one another. Show compassion to each others differences. Everyone's thoughts count and should be shown some respect. Also, there is confidentiality, "What's said in the group stays in the group." Of course in most cases there are snacks as well. You know what I envision when I hear of this. The last supper, or the many times you see Jesus with his closes disciples. Often they were eating, gathered around a table, sharing thoughts and discussing them. You see it in accountability meetings for addictions. It's amazing we still don't realize that this is important. However, none the less it's true.

Odds are based on the percentages of what I've experienced you are not a talker. If you are then you probably can name at least nine people around you who are not. Knowing this we have to begin to be willing to change this. You do not have to go from quiet to talkative. You simply must choose to be willing to communicate. This not only means speaking it means listening. It not only means listening, it means responding with action. We must show compassion to one another's differences and confidence in that which we are and be ok with feeling the way we do. We must be confident in who we are and yet be willing to look inside to see one another for who we are. Communication is not only externally important it is also internally important. We should not only be concerned with how and if we speak with others but also be concerned with the communication within ourselves. When you think about something, mulling it over are you optimistic or pessimistic? Do you often think I'm just not even going to think about that or do you dwell on it thinking the same thing over and over?

What I've come to notice is we often communicate externally, with others very similar to how we communicate internally with ourselves. In many persons, the ones who don't communicate externally with others, there is a lot of internal thought but it is never expressed outwardly. I've seen lots of these kinds of persons develop strong communication skills in the way expressed and described a moment ago in small group type settings. I'm not saying it's easy, I am saying I've seen and heard of the effective success of persons willing to communicate. The most difficult thing is that communication is two ways. When you hear about things communicating in electronics and equipment it is something that is being sent and received in two directions. We could all learn from that. Strange how we can build cars, computers and various things that require the very two way communication we ourselves seem unwilling, incapable or often just not interested in doing.

He/She doesn't _____, (Fill in the blank) so why should I try?

You know I often hear about this. However, have you ever known someone who was not good at something and got better because they were always being told how bad they were at it? I know guys in sports who have wanted to get better but their coaches only worked well with guys who could easily be told, do this and they did it and boom got better. If they had to be taught, that was different. I've seen lots of people who wanted to be better. They just needed someone who could teach them. Let's use math as an example. If the math teacher just keeps looking at them, grading their papers, giving them D's and F's and saying, "You just don't get it do you?" (Clearly they don't) "You'll never make above a C if you're lucky."

(Not if they aren't taught differently) What if that teacher stops teaching and instead just judges and gives up on trying? What if that child's parents do the same at home? What if instead they lead based on a method of communication and Loved in the way we've been discussing.

Let's say instead the child loves a certain sport, maybe its football. Each team has 11 players on the field. If either team is caught with an extra man on the field how many do they have. "Twelve" the child answers. And they were at their own 45 yard line. How many yards are they penalized? "Ten" the child answers. So now where are they located for the next play? "The 35 yard line" the child answers. It's not that the child doesn't know math. Instead, it was that he needed help in understanding. Using the spin of a football analogy to teach the trajectory and velocity in physics could be a very worth while idea for some! Then if the person begins to understand math in their own language it is possible they might be able to understand math in other ways as well.

My point is this. It's worth trying but you may have to adapt your communication style to be effective with in the capabilities of others and understand the interest of the person you are communicating to so that you open up the flow of two way travel, a two way signal versus it only going one way and even then possibly only being sent and not received. And let's not forget if it's not sent and received, results are highly unlikely.

An example:

One of my favorite movies is Days of Thunder. Colt is a race car driver and he is tearing up his car. He goes through turns to fast, going through tires too fast. He wrecks his car every race. His manager continues to express the need for him to do things differently. Colt has never raced these types of cars. After a fight, the owner finally tells the manager he has to figure a way to communicate and work with Colt or they will not obtain a sponsor and everyone will be out of work and potentially a lot of money that he invested. And so the manager walks into a bar where Colt is sitting. He begins to explain how if the car is loose in the rear end, Colt needs to tell him. If it's tight in the front, he needs to know. Colt explains that he can't. His manager replies with a confident, sure you can. Colt explains why he can not. He explains that he doesn't know what these terms mean, a turn here, tight there, or being loose. I'm an idiot he says, I don't know anything about cars!

Funny, when we first see Colt he is confident and sure of himself and his skills as a driver but when confronted with having to team up for success and having to communicate this turns into pride. This in turn causes failure, wrecked cars, yelling, burned up tires, and so forth. It is not until Colt can say, I don't get it, and his manager says, I'll teach you, let's learn from each other and work together, let's… communicate both ways that we see positive results. It's after this that we see trust, faith and success not just in wins on a race car track but in each individual character and in the relationships in the story.

CHAPTER 23

A love letter

I'd like to close this book by encouraging you to never stop seeking the truth about Love. When my life took it's true turning point it was when I was willing to seek out the truth about a word that had seemed to cause more pain and wrong in my life than good or right. I went to the Bible first. I remember praying, God I must know nothing about love. I have two failed marriages and one more very emotional long term relationship that have all ended with hurt. I don't want that again. I want not only to be loved differently but I want to love others differently. Show me the truth about love. And so he began to do his work. God is an amazing teacher. Just look at how Jesus taught during his short but amazing ministry on earth. I never liked it when I'd hear the phrase, the Bible is our love letter from God. In my new and current, yet humble opinion, it is instead if anything, if a letter at all it is a letter of Love from God. It is there for us to learn about his Love for us, how to Love him and how to Love one another as he intended from the beginning. He is teaching us about the initial idea of communication in Love, about various languages of Love.

You see as I did that research I found that I could not find a place where Love was not connected with action, often sacrifice and in many cases was clearly a choice and in some cases a command. Yet even when commanded we must choose to follow.

Experience-God so loved the world he sent his only begotten son....

Teaching of command via action-The greatest commandment is this, love God with all your mind and heart and soul and the second is the same to love others as yourself

Command-Men love your wives as Christ also loved the Church

Action-Jacob worked seven years to be with the woman he loved, and when her father didn't follow through with his part of the bargain, he worked seven more.

God doesn't command us to do what he isn't willing to do himself. He doesn't give rules/commands that are without purpose or without love. He does not tell us how to love and leave us wondering why. He shows us the why through others experiences, through those stories we see the result and stand in awe. So let us move forward in our actions that we'd have experiences and prove them with results in kind.

In the Bible verse 2 Corinthians 3:17 we read about how when our faces become unveiled we begin to be transformed. Have you been walking your life with a covering over your face? Maybe like a veil, able to get around but so much of life being unclear and fuzzy? It is my hope that those reading this would have their eyes unveiled to see things in a new way and that their minds be renewed and the word Love, Redefined

The Final Page

I recently had an, ah ha moment. You know, when you're like, "Whoa, that's what that means!" I've often heard the phrases, Freedom in Jesus or Freedom in God. And even having been somewhat involved in Christianity in some way since I was little I don't think I ever fully got how a religion that teaches about a whole lot of things we can't do gives us freedom.

Then I realized, much of the freedom comes from when we move in the timelines and power of the one who created this world, with a God who is over all, sees all and knows all. When we are defined not by the world's time but by a God who is beyond time; when we are defined within God's purpose and not our own purpose of being married, having children, living in the big city, having the nice house and car or making it to president of the big corporation or living whatever dream we have; when we follow a God who is bigger than our time, our timelines, our purposes and let him do his work, that is quite freeing.

The neat thing I've noticed along the way is we still often get to enjoy His grace as he allows us to have dreams and fulfill them, just a little different or in some cases a lot differently than how we had laid out our plans for ourselves. Freedom in Faith in God could also likely be defined as Freedom in the Love of God. Now that we've taken a deeper look at the definition of love, I hope you will not only see it redefined but that you might also see God redefined also.

Thanks...

I'd like to especially thank Ken and Tim Taylor. They were the catalyst in my walk to both seeing love in action and helping me see its true definition. They always made me welcome so that I could be introduced to the possibility of living a life different than the one I lived prior to knowing them.

I'd also, thank you for reading this and being willing to see, Love Redefined.

And a thank you to those who helped to teach me about redefining love and renewing how we think, Gary Chapman, Steve Brown, Dr. Wayne Dyer, and many, many others.

Love Redefined – Experiences on going/Written from 3/2007-3/2009

www.bradlywilliams.com

www.ingramcontent.com/pod-product-compliance
Lightning Source LLC
La Vergne TN
LVHW011201080426
835508LV00007B/533